BIG ENGLISH 3 PLUS

Mario Herrera • Christopher Sol Cruz

STUDENT'S BOOK

Contents

Unit	Vocabulary	Structures
1 Wake Up! pp. 4–19	**Daily routines:** do my homework, eat breakfast, get dressed, go home, go to school, go to the park, play soccer, play video games, wake up, watch TV **Times:** seven fifty-five, seven forty-five, seven thirty, in the afternoon, evening, morning	What does (he) do before/after school? He eats before/after school. When does he get dressed? He gets dressed at seven ten. I always/usually/often/sometimes/never eat eggs.
2 A Lot of Jobs! pp. 20–35	**Jobs:** cashier, farmer, firefighter, nurse, police officer, scientist, student, waiter **Places:** farm, fire station, hospital, laboratory, police station, restaurant, store, college	What does (he) do? He's a nurse. Where does (she) work? She works (on a farm). They play music every day. Does he live on Park Street? Yes, he does./No, he doesn't. They don't wear suits to work.
3 Working Hard! pp. 36–51	**Chores:** clean my room, do the dishes, feed the fish, make my bed, practice the piano, study for a test, take out the trash, walk the dog **Adverbs of frequency:** always, never, usually, sometimes	I (always) make my bed. What do (we) have to do? We have to (make our bed). You like/love/hate sleeping. Does he like/love/hate playing? I don't like/love/hate cleaning up.
Checkpoint Units 1–3 pp. 52–55	**Units 1–3 Exam Preparation pp. 56–57**	
4 Amazing Animals pp. 58–73	**Animals:** bear, camel, deer, lizard, owl, penguin, sea lion, shark, toucan **Habitats:** desert, forest, ice and snow, jungle, lake, mountain, ocean, rain forest	What can (bears) do? They can climb, but they can't talk. What can you do? I can/can't run. quiet – quietly good – well
5 Wonderful Weather! pp. 74–89	**Weather:** cloudy, cold, cool, hot, rainy, snowy, sunny, warm, windy **Clothes:** coat, raincoat, sandals, scarf, shorts, sunglasses, sweater today, yesterday	What's the weather like today? It's (hot and sunny). What was the weather like yesterday? It was (windy). I wasn't hot. We weren't cold. We were/weren't freezing. Was she late? Yes, she was./No, she wasn't.
6 Smells Good! pp. 90–105	**Verb senses:** feels, looks, sounds, tastes, smells **Adjectives:** awful, beautiful, delicious, good, horrible, nice, soft, sweet, terrible, tight	How does the apple pie taste? It tastes (delicious). The milkshake tastes sweet. The shoes feel smooth.
Checkpoint Units 4–6 pp. 106–109	**Units 4–6 Exam Preparation pp. 110–111**	
7 Fabulous Food! pp. 112–127	**Food:** bread, cucumbers, green peppers, lettuce, mushrooms, mustard, olives, onions, tomato sauce, turkey	Is there any (bread)? Yes, there is./No, there isn't. There are some (peppers). There aren't any (peppers). He has some/a lot of/a little meat. You have some/a lot of/a few potatoes. How much fruit?/How many onions?
8 Healthy Living pp. 128–143	**Healthy living:** eat/have breakfast, eat/have a healthy lunch, drink water, get any exercise, get (enough) sleep, ride a bike	Did (you) get enough sleep yesterday? Yes, I did./No, I didn't. They walked. She saw a film.
9 School Trips! pp. 144–159	**Places:** aquarium, art gallery, concert hall, dairy farm, national park, science museum, theater, zoo **Verbs:** ate, got, had, learned, saw, walked, was, went, were, liked	Where did (they) go? They went to the (zoo). What did he see? He saw sharks. I didn't go to the theater. They didn't see any actors.
Checkpoint Units 7–9 pp. 160–163	**Units 7–9 Exam Preparation pp. 164–165**	

Wordlist pp. 166–169   **Big English Song** p. 170

CLIL/Culture	Writing	Phonics	Values	I can...
Science: Keeping clean bacteria, cough, decay, germs, gum disease, health, healthy, sick, skin, sneeze, sweat **Around the World: Time zones** chat, dark, different, e-pals, globe, half-turn, map, online, Time Zone	Sentence: Subjects and Verbs	a_e, i_e, o_e cake, face, game, shape bike, like, time, ride bone, home, note	Do your chores.	...talk about what people do before and after school. ...talk about different times of the day. ...talk about keeping clean. ...find and use adverbs of frequency, subjects, and verbs.
Social Science: Creative jobs create, drawings, galleries, materials, paintings, photo shoot, piece of art, professional, sculptures, unusual **Around the World: Communities** be proud of, collect, community, contest, donate, get lost, trash	Sentence: Two Subjects and Verbs	sm, st, sp, sk smart, smile, smoke star, stop, storm space, Spain, spoon skates, ski, skin	Respect others.	...talk about what people do and where they work. ...talk about creative jobs. ...find and use two subjects and two verbs.
Math: Pocket money adult, cash, clean, cost, earn, let (someone) know, save, stranger, wash **Around the World: Work** business, entrance, noodles, share, shovel, sidewalk, task, tiring	Paragraph: Titles	ay, oy day, May, pay, ray, say, way boy, joy, soy, toy	Always be happy to help.	...talk about how often people do things. ...talk about what people like/don't like doing and have to do. ...talk about chores and pocket money. ...use capital letters in titles.
Science: Camouflage blend in, bottom of the ocean, desert, rain forest, stone, surroundings, tree bark **Around the World: Pets** alligators, canaries, geckos, goldfish, parakeets, rodents, snakes, tarantulas	Paragraph: Topic Sentences	ea, oi, oe bean, eat, meat peach, sea, tea boil, coin, oil foe, toe	Protect animals and their habitats.	...talk about what animals can/can't do and where they're found. ...find and use adverbs. ...find and use topic sentences.
Geography: Climate average, climate, degrees Celsius, desert, dry, extreme, mild, minus **Around the World: Weather** cricket, fill up, kite, sledding, snowball fight	Paragraph: Detail Sentences	sc, sw, sn, sl scar, scarf, scout swan, sweet, swim snack, snail, snow sleep, slim, slow	Prepare for the weather.	...talk about the weather today and in the past. ...talk about clothes. ...talk about climates around the world. ...find and use detail sentences.
Science: Animal senses avoid, brain, danger, echo, information, senses, sound waves, taste buds, tongue **Around the World: Jobs** clean, awful, fresh, smelly, stink, take care of, wet	Paragraph: Final Sentences	fl, pl, gl, bl flag, flip-flops, fly plant, play, plum glad, glass, glow black, block, blow	Try new things.	...describe how things look, feel, taste, smell, or sound. ...talk about the five senses in people and animals. ...find and use final sentences.
Science: Vitamins blood, bone, brain, energy, fat/water, healthy, iron, muscle, skin, soluble, teeth, vitamin **Around the World: Breakfasts** blueberries, hard-boiled/fried eggs, cereal, donut, honey, oats, porridge, toast	Paragraphs	br, cr, dr, fr, gr, pr, tr bread, brick cream, cry dream, drive frog, from grass, green train, troll	Try different foods.	...ask and answer about food. ...talk about vitamins and how they help my body. ...find different parts of a paragraph.
P.E.: Keeping healthy active, activities, body, burn, calorie, in shape, measure, put on, rest, weight **Around the World: Strange sports** contest, court, diving, net, puck, race, regatta, rowing, scuba, team	Combining Sentences with *and*, *but*, *or*	all, au, aw all, ball, call, tall, wall haul, Paul claw, draw, law, yawn	Get exercise.	...talk about healthy and unhealthy habits. ...ask and answer about activities in the past. ...use *and*, *or*, and *but* in sentences.
Art: Paintings artist, colorful, funny, happy, impressionist, oil painting, painter, sad, sketch, strange, watercolor **Around the World: Stage performances** dramatic, entertainment, flamenco, open-air theater, performance, play, popular, puppet, show, stage	Writing Sentences	nt, ld, nd, st ant, plant, tent child, cold, old band, hand, sand chest, fast, nest	Recognize your talents.	...talk about actions in the past and places to visit. ...talk about paintings. ...write sentences with a subject, verb, and object.

unit 1 Wake Up!

1 Listen, look, and say.

Monday, May 13th

1 wake up
2 eat breakfast
3 get dressed
4 go to school
5 go home
6 go to the park
7 play soccer
8 do my homework
9 play video games
10 watch TV

2 Listen, find, and say.

3 Play a game.

4 Listen and sing. Does Kate eat breakfast?

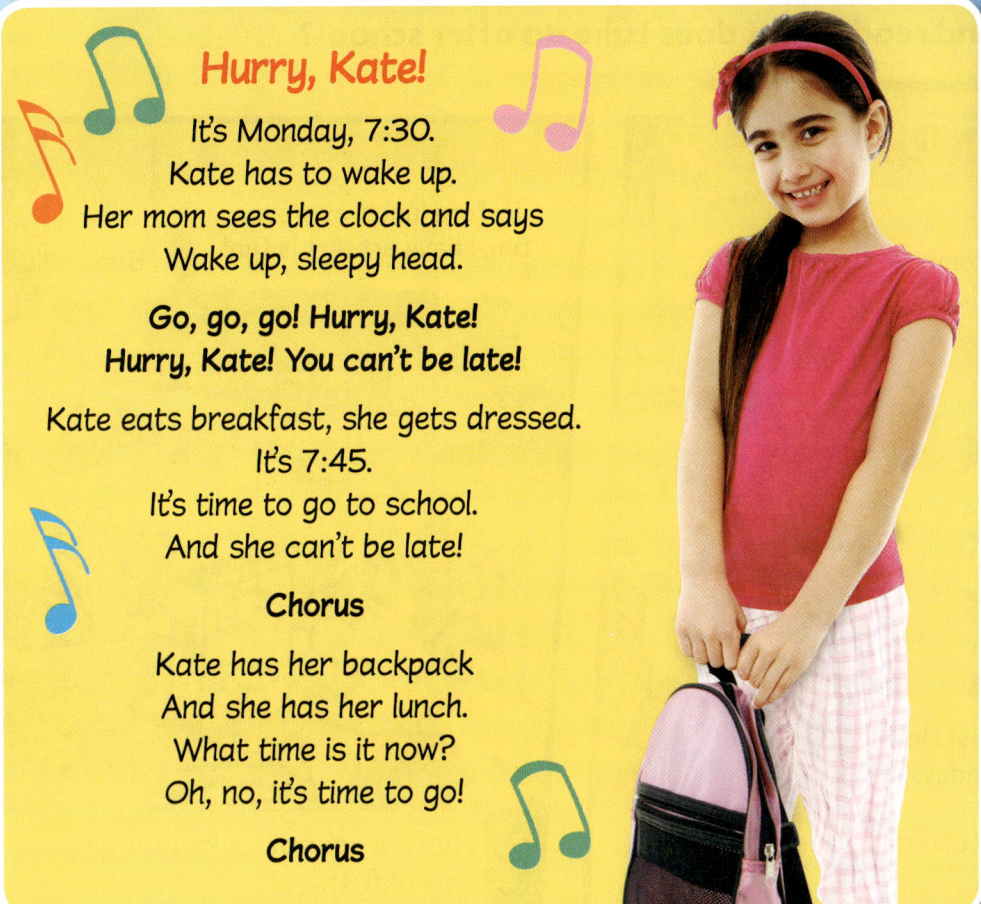

Hurry, Kate!

It's Monday, 7:30.
Kate has to wake up.
Her mom sees the clock and says
Wake up, sleepy head.

**Go, go, go! Hurry, Kate!
Hurry, Kate! You can't be late!**

Kate eats breakfast, she gets dressed.
It's 7:45.
It's time to go to school.
And she can't be late!

Chorus

Kate has her backpack
And she has her lunch.
What time is it now?
Oh, no, it's time to go!

Chorus

5 Read, match, and say. Ask and answer.

1	7:00	a	seven forty-five
2	7:30	b	seven fifty-five
3	7:45	c	seven o'clock
4	7:55	d	seven thirty
5	4:45	e	five twenty-five
6	4:00	f	four forty-five
7	8:15	g	four o'clock
8	5:25	h	eight fifteen

When does she wake up?

She wakes up at seven o'clock.

 Which activities do you do inside? Which do you do outside?

Story

 6 Listen and read. What does Luke do after school?

1 Luke wakes up and goes into the kitchen.

2 Before school, Luke always eats breakfast.

3 After breakfast, he brushes his teeth. Then he washes his face.

4 He gets dressed.

5 He puts on his shoes. He's ready for school.

6 But there's no school today!

7 Read and say before school or after school.

1 Luke eats breakfast.
2 Luke gets dressed.
3 Luke plays soccer.
4 Luke puts on his shoes.
5 Luke wakes up.
6 Luke plays basketball.

THINK BIG Do you like Mondays? Why/Why not?
What different things do you do on different days?

Language in Action

8 Listen and look at the sentences. Help Luke and Amy make more.

get dressed   do my homework

7:20   2:15   in the morning/afternoon/evening

When does he go to school ?
He goes to school at 8:10 .
When does she go home ?
She goes home in the afternoon .

9 Read and match. Make sentences with a partner.

1 Sam eats breakfast at 7:30
2 Jack wakes up at
3 Paula gets
4 Esteban does his homework in
5 Sandra plays video
6 Alice watches

a games at 5:00 in the afternoon.
b in the morning.
c TV at 8:00 in the evening.
d dressed at 7:50 in the morning.
e 6:45 in the morning.
f the afternoon.

10 Look at 9. Ask and answer.

When does Paula get dressed?

She gets dressed at seven fifty.

8 Unit 1 language practice (*When does he go to school? He goes to school at eight ten.*)

Language in Action

 11 **Listen and find the clocks.**

a  b

c  d

12 **What does Claudia do before and after school? Make sentences.**

Claudia's Schedule

6:30 wake up

3:20 go home

7:00 get dressed

6:45 get up

3:30 ride my bike

5:30 play soccer

4:45 do my homework

7:15 eat breakfast

6:30 eat dinner

7:30 go to school

13 **Look at 12. What does Claudia do in the morning, afternoon, and evening?**

 Claudia wakes up at 6:30 in the morning.

She plays soccer in the afternoon.

language practice (*Claudia wakes up at 6:30 in the morning.*) Unit 1 **9**

Content Connection | Science

14 Read and choose. Discuss with a partner.

Why do we brush our teeth?
 a to make them white
 b to get rid of food
 c to keep them strong

15 Listen and read. What are bacteria? Then check your answer in 14.

Keep It Clean!

CONTENT WORDS
bacteria   cough   decay   germs
gum disease   health   healthy
sick   skin   sneeze   sweat

Question: Why is it important to shower, brush my teeth, and wash my hands?
Max, 10

Taking a Shower

People shower to look and feel good but also to keep clean and healthy. We can't always see it with our eyes, but we get dirty all the time. We use warm water and soap to wash away sweat, dead skin, and bacteria. Bacteria are tiny things that live on our skin. They can sometimes make us sick, so make sure you wash your whole body well.

Brushing Your Teeth

We brush our teeth to keep them strong and healthy. It's good to do this after every meal, but most people brush them twice a day: once in the morning after breakfast and once at night before going to bed. Brushing our teeth for about two minutes cleans away bacteria that can cause tooth decay and gum disease.

Washing Your Hands

Washing your hands is also very important. Every day our hands pick up millions of germs that can make us sick. Washing them with soap and water for at least 20 seconds gets rid of germs. Wash your hands before you eat, after you go to the bathroom, after you cough or sneeze, and any other time they get dirty.

THINK BIG What other things can you do to stay healthy?
Where can we learn about staying healthy?

16 **Look at 15. Read and say true or false.**

1. We shower to wash away bacteria from our body.
2. Sometimes we are dirty, but we can't see it.
3. There are no bacteria in our mouth.
4. Brushing our teeth after every meal causes gum disease.
5. We pick up germs when we touch things with our hands.
6. Germs can't make you sick.

17 **What do you do every morning? Put the activities in order. Then compare with a partner.**

a Brush teeth
b Brush hair
c Take a shower
d Clean ears
e Get dressed
f Have breakfast
g Wash hands
h Go to the bathroom

When do you brush your teeth?

I brush my teeth after breakfast and before I go to sleep.

PROJECT

18 **Make a Keep It Clean poster. Then present it to the class.**

Eat healthy food.

Brush your teeth twice a day. It keeps them clean and healthy.

I eat healthy food, and I brush my teeth twice a day.

Grammar

19 **Look, listen, and point. Then say.**

a  I often have fruit for breakfast. I sometimes have watermelon. I never have cereal for breakfast.

b  I always eat cereal for breakfast. I usually drink juice, too. I never eat eggs for breakfast.

I **always** eat cereal. *****
I **usually** drink juice. ****
I **often** have fruit. ***
I **sometimes** eat bread. *
I **never** eat eggs.

He **always** eats breakfast.
Does he **always** eat breakfast?
He doesn't **always** eat breakfast.
BUT
He **sometimes** eats/doesn't eat eggs.
Sometimes he eats/doesn't eat eggs.
He eats/doesn't eat eggs **sometimes**.

20 **Look at 19. Complete the sentences.**

How often do you

... drink milk with your breakfast?

1 I ? drink milk with my breakfast! Milk is good! *****
   (Sam, 9)
2 I don't like milk very much. I ? eat yogurt. ****
   (Trish, 10)

... eat eggs for breakfast?

3 I ? eat eggs for breakfast. They're OK. *
   (Nathan, 10)
4 I ? eat eggs for breakfast. I don't like eggs!
   (Sonia, 10)

... eat fruit for breakfast?

5 I ? eat fruit but not every day. *
   (Bea, 10)
6 I ? drink fresh orange juice. It's the same, isn't it? ***
   (Jordan, 9)

Grammar

21 Look at the chart. Ask and answer.

	*****	****	***	*	
Chloe	get up at 7 a.m.		watch TV after school		
Mario		take the bus to school			
Peter				play online games with his friends	go to bed after 10 p.m.
Eva	eat a salad for lunch				

1. Chloe/often/get up at 8 a.m.?
2. Mario/always/walk to school?
3. Peter/usually/play computer games on his own?
4. Eva/often/eat pasta for lunch?
5. Chloe/usually/do her homework after school?
6. Peter/sometimes/go to bed after 10 p.m.?

> Does Chloe often get up at 8 a.m.?

> No, she doesn't. She always gets up at 7 a.m.

22 Read and choose the correct answer.

1. Do you watch TV?
   a I don't usually watch TV.
   b I often don't watch TV.
   c I don't watch sometimes TV.
2. Do you always go to bed at 9 p.m.?
   a Often I don't go to bed that early.
   b I don't always go to bed that early.
   c I don't go to bed that early always.
3. Do you like soda?
   a Always I don't drink soda.
   b I don't drink never soda.
   c I don't often drink soda.
4. What do you do when you're sick?
   a I don't go usually to school.
   b Always I don't go to school.
   c Sometimes I don't go to school.

23 Look, read, and write.

On weekdays, ¹ ? at 7 a.m. and get ready for school. ² ? breakfast with my mom and my brother. ³ ? breakfast with us. He's a doctor, and ⁴ ? for work very early. How about you? ⁵ ? breakfast with your family? What ⁶ ? for breakfast?

1	I	get up	always
2	I	have	usually
3	Dad	not have	always
4	he	leave	sometimes
5	you	have	always
6	you	have	usually

grammar (He always eats breakfast.) Unit 1 **13**

Culture Connection | Around the World

Time Zones

1   Look at your watch. What time is it now? Is it the same for everyone around the world? No, it isn't. That's because the world is divided into time zones. Look at the globe to find out why. When it's light in Hong Kong (A), it's still dark in New York (B). In fact, it isn't even the same day! This happens because the earth makes a half-turn in 12 hours, so New York sees the new day 12 hours after Hong Kong. When it's 8:00 on Monday morning in Hong Kong, it's still 8:00 on Sunday evening in New York!

2   Sometimes there are different time zones in the same country. Look at the map of the United States. Because it's a very big country, it has four different time zones.

24 Look at the globe. Why is it daytime in some countries and nighttime in others?

25 🎧14 Listen and read. Where do the children live?

> **CONTENT WORDS**
> chat   dark   different   e-pals   globe   half-turn   map   online   time zone

26 Look at **25**. Read and choose.

1   When it's daytime in Hong Kong, it's **daytime/nighttime** in New York.
2   In Hong Kong, the day starts 12 hours **before/after** it starts in New York.
3   Hong Kong and New York are in the same **time zone/day** for only 12 hours.
4   There are different time zones in different parts of **all/some** countries.
5   For Marcus, the day changes **before/after** it changes for Maria.
6   Kara goes to bed **before/after** everyone else.

14   Unit 1

Maria

Marcus

John

Kara

3   These four e-pals live in different parts of the country. Let's say it's 10:30 a.m. for Kara in California. She's in class. She isn't hungry yet because she always has a good breakfast. In Montana, it's 11:30 a.m., and John is already thinking about lunch. He's hungry, and he can't wait for the long break! For Maria, in Texas, it's 12:30 p.m. She and her friends are eating sandwiches for lunch. It's 1:30 p.m. in Washington, D.C., and Marcus is putting his empty lunchbox into his bag. He's getting ready for his afternoon class.

4   The four friends have the same bedtime. They often chat online in the evenings, but they need to make sure that the time is right for everyone!

27 Talk with a partner. These people live in different time zones. What do you think they're doing right now?

1 Emma – Anchorage, Alaska: Sunday 10:15 a.m.
2 Carlos – Mexico City, Mexico: Sunday 13:15 p.m.
3 Sophia – Greece, Athens: Sunday 9:15 p.m.
4 Jin – Beijing, China: Monday 2:15 a.m.

a having dinner at a restaurant
b having lunch at home
c having breakfast with all the family
d sleeping

> I think Emma's having breakfast with her family. It's Sunday, and they're all at home.

> Or she's sleeping. I never get up before 11 a.m. on a Sunday!

THINK BIG It's ten o'clock in the morning where you are. Find out what time it is in Buenos Aires, Cairo, and Sydney.

culture connection (time zones) Unit 1 **15**

Writing | Sentence: Subjects and Verbs

28 **Read and find.**

> A sentence has a *subject* and a *verb*.
> *She* *eats* breakfast before school.

1 I ride my bike to school.

29 **Find the subjects and verbs. Compare with your partner.**

1 Andrew eats lunch at 12:30.
2 Marcia goes to school at 8:05.
3 We go home at 3:50 in the afternoon.
4 My brother does his homework at 4:30.
5 You eat dinner with your family in the evening.

30 **What's missing, subject or verb? Make new sentences and compare with a partner.**

1 Bridget ? at 6:45 in the morning.
2 ? eats breakfast at 7:00.
3 Her ? goes to the park with friends.
4 Beth ? after school with her family.
5 ? get dressed in the morning.

31 **Read about Jack's day. Change all the information in *blue* and *red*. Write a new paragraph.**

Jack *wakes up* at six ten in the morning. *He* *takes a shower* and gets dressed before school. *He* rides a bike to school and gets there at eight o'clock. *His brother* gets to school at eight ten. *Jack* *plays soccer* after school in the park. *He* *does his homework* at five fifteen. The family eats dinner together and then they *watch TV*.

32 **Write four sentences about your day. Read them to your partner.**

a_e, i_e, o_e | Phonics

 33 Listen, read, and repeat.

1 a_e   2 i_e   3 o_e

 34 Listen and find. Then say.

face   bike   bone

 35 Listen and blend the sounds.

1 g-a-me   game
3 t-i-me   time
5 h-o-me   home
7 r-i-de   ride

2 c-a-ke   cake
4 n-o-te   note
6 sh-a-pe   shape
8 l-i-ke   like

 36 Read aloud. Then listen and chant.

What time is it?
It's time to play a game.
What time is it?
It's time to eat cake.
What time is it?
It's time to ride a bike.
What time is it?
It's time to go home.

phonics (a_e, i_e, o_e) Unit 1

Values | Do your chores.

37 Look, listen, and point.

a
I feed the dog before school.

b
I clean my room after school.

c
I wash the dishes after dinner.

PROJECT

38 What chores do you do at home? Copy the chart in your notebook and ✓. Then ask three classmates about their chores.

Review

39 Read and choose.

¹**When/What** does Mia wake up on Friday? She ²**wakes/wake** up at seven fifteen because she takes a shower, gets dressed, eats breakfast, and brushes her teeth ³**before/after** school. She goes to school ⁴**at/in** eight o'clock. School finishes at three thirty in the ⁵**morning/afternoon**. When ⁶**do/does** she do her homework? At four fifteen. Then she goes ⁷**to/at** the park and ⁸**plays/playing** baseball with her friends.

40 Make five sentences in your notebook about things you do or don't do before and after school. Use **always**, **usually**, **often**, **sometimes**, or **never**.

41 Play the **Silly Sentences** game.

I Can

- talk about what people do before and after school.
- talk about different times of the day.
- talk about keeping clean.
- find and use adverbs of frequency, subjects, and verbs.

unit 2 A Lot of Jobs!

1 Listen, look, and say.

Different Jobs

 1 firefighter

 2 police officer

 3 cashier

 4 waiter

 5 farmer

 6 scientist

 7 nurse

 8 student

2 Listen, find, and say.

3 Play a game.

4 Listen and sing. How many jobs are in the song?

Working Together

There are many people
In our community.
So many jobs to do,
So many places to be.

**Working together, working hard.
Nurse, farmer, teacher, and chef.**

Where does she work?
What does she do?
She's a nurse,
And she always helps you.

Chorus
Where does he work?
What does he do?
He's a firefighter,
And he's very brave, too.

5 Match the jobs in 1 to the places. Make sentences.

a  at a hospital

b  at a store

c  at a fire station

d  at a college

e  at a laboratory

f  at a police station

g  at a restaurant

h  on a farm

A student studies at a college.

A scientist works at a laboratory.

THINK BIG What job is this?
"I sometimes work at night. I sometimes work in the day.
I wear a uniform. I often work with another person."

Story

 6 Listen and read. What does Luke's mom do?

1 Luke and his dad are at the hospital.

2 They want to find Luke's mom.

3 Luke's mom is at work.

4 Luke's mom works at the hospital.

5 Luke's mom isn't a doctor or a nurse.

6 Luke's mom is a cashier. She works at a gift shop. It's her birthday today!

7 **Read and complete the sentences. Then say.**
1 Luke is looking for his ❓.
2 Luke's mom works at the ❓.
3 Luke's mom isn't a doctor or a ❓.
4 Luke's mom is a ❓.
5 Today it's Luke's mom's ❓.

 **What other people work in a hospital?
What do they do?
What do you think makes a good nurse?**

Language in Action

8 Listen and look at the sentences. Help Luke and Amy make more.

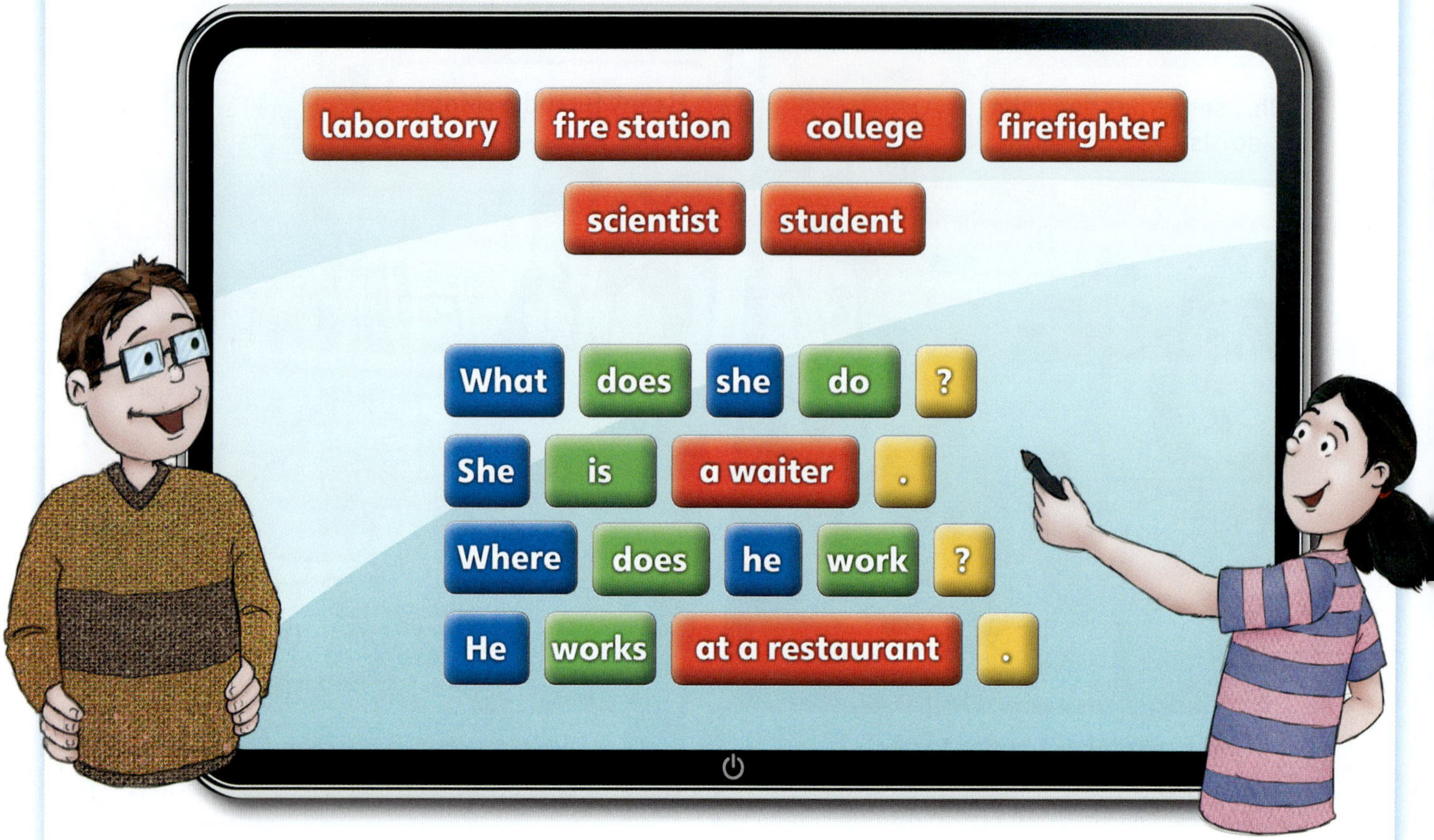

laboratory fire station college firefighter
scientist student

What does she do?
She is a waiter.
Where does he work?
He works at a restaurant.

9 Put the dialog in order with a partner. Then change the words in red and make new dialogs.

a **She** works **at a school**.
b What does your **mom** do?
c **She's** a **nurse**.
d Where does **she** work?

10 What about you? Ask and answer about your family.

What does your dad do? — He's a farmer.
Where does he work? — He works on a farm.

Unit 2 language practice (*What does he do? He's a farmer.*)

Language in Action

11 **Listen and match.**

a

b

c

1 Megan

2 Susan

3 Ellie

12 **Read and choose.**
1 **What/Why** does your grandpa do? He's a cashier, and he works in a gift shop.
2 **When/Where** do Paul and Leyla study? They study at college.
3 Where **do/does** Alice work? She works at a fire station.
4 What do you **do/does**? I'm a doctor.
5 I work **on/in** a farm. I'm a farmer.
6 We work **at/on** a hospital.

13 **Look and make questions and answers.**
1 a what/brothers/do?
      scientists
   b where/work?
      laboratory
2 a what/you/do?
      teacher
   b where/work?
      school
3 a what/mom/do?
      firefighter
   b where/she/work?
      fire station

What do your brothers do?

They're scientists.

language practice (*Where do they work? They work at a school.*) Unit 2

Content Connection | Social Science

14 Discuss with a partner.

> What do you enjoy doing?

> I like drawing. It makes me feel happy.

15 Listen and read. Which of these people sell their work to magazines?

The Work Files: Creative Jobs

CONTENT WORDS
create   drawings   galleries
materials   paintings   photo shoot
piece of art   professional
sculptures   unusual

People spend a big part of their lives at work, so it's very important to choose the right job. When you do something you really enjoy, you feel happy. Today we're taking a look at creative jobs. Would you like to do one of them?

Artist

Professional artists usually go to art school. They learn to use different materials to create a work of art. They use pencils to make drawings, oil paints, acrylics, or water colors to make paintings, and metal or wood to make other works of art. Some artists like to work with unusual materials like chewing gum, buttons, or plastic supermarket bags! Artists show their work in art galleries. A work of art can be very expensive.

Photographer

Photographers travel a lot and take pictures of people and places all over the world. Their work is sometimes difficult or dangerous, like when they take pictures of wild animals. Serious photographers never go out without their camera. They don't want to miss a good picture. They sell their pictures to websites, newspapers, magazines, and television news shows. They also sell books with their pictures.

Fashion Designer

Fashion designers create the clothes we wear. First, they draw sketches with their ideas. Then they cut patterns to make dresses, pants, coats, and many more things. Designing clothes can be a lot of fun. Fashion designers show their work in fashion shows or do photo shoots for magazines. They sell their clothes in stores or online.

> **THINK BIG** What other creative jobs can you think of?
> What talents do you need to do a creative job?

26   Unit 2

16 Look at **15**. Read and complete. Use the words from the box.

> camera   happy   pattern   sketch   unusual   world

1. When you like your job, you feel ?.
2. Chewing gum is a(n) ? material to use for a work of art.
3. Photographers often travel all over the ? for their work.
4. Photographers like to have their ? with them all the time.
5. When they have a good idea, fashion designers draw a ?.
6. Clothes are cut using a ?.

17 Interview a partner. Take notes in your notebook. Share with the class.

1. Do you like art? Do you have a favorite work of art?
2. What kinds of pictures do you like to look at (wild animals, fashion, etc.)?
3. Do you like fashion? What kinds of clothes do you usually wear?

PROJECT

18 Make a **Creative Job** presentation. Then present it to the class.

Notes
Answer the questions:
What's his/her job?
What does he/she do?
Does he/she have a special talent?
Is he/she happy with his/her job? Why?
Find pictures to show the class.

Mark Willows is a video game designer. He creates video games. He knows a lot about computers.

He's very happy with his job because it's fun!

Grammar

 19 Listen and read. What's the man's job?

At the Oscars...

Reporter: Can you answer some questions, please?
Man: Who, me? OK.
Reporter: Where do you live?
Man: I live on Park Street.
Reporter: What sports do you play?
Man: I play basketball. Um... Excuse me. Do I know you?
Reporter: No, but I know you. You're one of the actors.
Man: No, I'm not.
Reporter: But you're wearing a black suit!
Man: I always wear a black suit to work! I'm a waiter!

I **wear** a black suit to work.	**What do** you **wear** to work?
He **lives** on Park Street.	**Where does** he **live**?
She **plays** music every day.	**When does** she **play** music?
They **like** listening to music.	**Why do** they **have** earphones?

Do I **wear** a black suit to work?	Yes, I do./No, I don't.
Does he **live** on Park Street?	Yes, he does./No, he doesn't.
Does she **play** music every day?	Yes, she does./No, she doesn't.
Do they **like** listening to music?	Yes, they do./No, they don't.

I **don't wear** a black suit to work.
He **doesn't live** on Park Street.
She **doesn't play** music every day.
They **don't like** listening to music.

Grammar

20 Read and complete.

1. Dan ? cartoons on TV on Saturday morning. (watch)
2. ? they ? their car on the weekend? (wash)
3. Jack ? his black bag everywhere. (carry)
4. My parents ? in an office. (not work)
5. ? Patrick ? on Vine Street? (live)
6. Maria ? her hair every day. (not brush)

21 Correct the sentences using the words in parentheses.

1. Mehmet works in a hospital. (office)
   Mehmet ? in a hospital. He ?
2. The twins play baseball. (basketball)
   The twins ?
3. He sees his grandpa every weekend. (every month)
   He ?
4. You live in New York. (Seattle)
   I ?
5. He knows a famous actor. (famous TV chef)
   He ?
6. The players wear red T-shirts. (blue T-shirts)
   The players ?

22 Complete the questions and answers.

1. Brad/star ✓
   Does Brad ? in a new movie?
   Yes, he ?.
2. they/ask ✗
   ? you questions?
   ?
3. you/cook ✓
   ? ?
   ?
4. Ann/wear ✗
   ? a uniform to work?
   ?
5. they/go ✓
   ? to school?
   ?
6. your friend/watch ✗
   ? sports on TV?
   ?

grammar (*Where does she live? She lives on Park Street.*) Unit 2

Culture Connection | Around the World

Making Communities Better

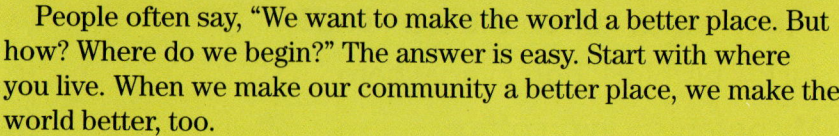

1   People often say, "We want to make the world a better place. But how? Where do we begin?" The answer is easy. Start with where you live. When we make our community a better place, we make the world better, too.
These children know this, and they're happy to do something about it. Let's meet them and see what they do. Maybe we can get some ideas to help our communities, too.

2   Lalana lives in Chiang Mai, Thailand. She knows that many schools in her city don't have money to buy books. Lalana and her friends ask people to donate books. They collect the books and take them to schools in their city. Many schools now have more and better books, thanks to Lalana and her friends.

Lalana

23 Discuss in groups.

Do you live in a big or a small community? What's it like?
What do you like about the place?
What do you like about the people?

24 Listen and read. Who helps tourists in their city?

> **CONTENT WORDS**
> be proud of   collect   community   contest
> donate   get lost   trash

25 Look at 24. Correct the mistakes. Write new sentences.

1 We don't change the world when we do things for our community.
2 In Chiang Mai, schools donate books to people.
3 Barcelona doesn't have many tourists.
4 Tourists say bad things about Carla's city when they go back home.
5 Marcus rides his bike to school.
6 Marcus and his friends pick up the trash, but they don't enjoy it.

30 Unit 2

3   Marcus lives in a small town near Melbourne, Australia. Every morning he walks to school. He sees a lot of trash along the road. He and his friends have a contest. They pick up the trash, and they see who can collect the most. They clean up the streets, and they have fun, too.

4   Carla lives in Barcelona, Spain. A lot of tourists visit her city every year, and they often get lost. Carla likes helping people, and she's proud of her city. On the weekends, she and her big sister help tourists find the places they're looking for. When the tourists go back home, they tell their friends that Barcelona is a wonderful place!

5   See? It isn't difficult. When every one of us does one little thing for our community, we make it a great place to live in.

26 Talk with a partner. What can you do to help? Choose from **a–d**. Do you have any other ideas?

1 Some old people live alone. They have no family, and they can't go out.
2 Some younger children in your school aren't very good students.
3 Some people don't have a job or a home. They live on the streets, and they have no money.
4 Your town is beautiful, but it doesn't have many visitors because people don't know about it.

a Ask supermarkets to donate the food they can't sell.
b Make a webpage with pictures and information about your town.
c Do their shopping for them.
d Help them with their lessons.

27 Write in your notebook three ways you can help your community.

 Present your ideas in **27** to the class. Then vote to decide on the best three ways you can help your community.

culture connection (communities) Unit 2   **31**

Writing | Two Subjects and Verbs

28 Read and find.

> A sentence can have two subjects and two verbs.
> Al is a farmer. Matt is a farmer.
> Al and Matt are farmers.
> I live in Rome. I work in Rome.
> I live and work in Rome.

1 Julie and John are students. They live and study at college.

29 Write the sentences. Use and to make two subjects or two verbs.

1 I live in a town. I work in a town.
2 Asya is a scientist. Alfonzo is a scientist.
3 My mother is a firefighter. My father is a firefighter.
4 I work at a restaurant. I eat at a restaurant.
5 My cousin lives in London. My cousin studies in London.
6 My sister lives on a farm. My brother lives on a farm.

30 Complete the sentences for you. Then say.

1 Before school, I ❓.
2 After school, I ❓.

Before school, I eat breakfast and get dressed.

After school, I play soccer and do my homework.

sm, st, sp, sk | Phonics

 31 Listen, read, and repeat.

1 **sm**   2 **st**   3 **sp**   4 **sk**

 32 Listen and find. Then say.

smile   **st**op   **sp**oon   **sk**ates

 33 Listen and blend the sounds.

1 s-m-ar-t   smart   2 s-k-i-n   skin
3 S-p-ai-n   Spain   4 s-m-o-ke   smoke
5 s-k-i   ski   6 s-t-or-m   storm
7 s-t-ar   star   8 s-p-a-ce   space

34 Read aloud. Then listen and chant.

Stop and look.
Look at the stars,
The stars in space,
And smile!

phonics (*sm, st, sp, sk*) Unit 2   **33**

Values | Respect others.

 35 Look, listen, and point.

a

b

c

PROJECT

 36 Make a class book about respecting others.

Review

 43

37 **Listen and say yes or no.**

1 Julie's mom works at a hospital.
2 Her mom is a doctor.
3 Her dad is a student.
4 Her sisters work on a farm.

38 **Make questions. Then say.**

1 I'm a firefighter.
2 My brother works at a laboratory.
3 My dad is a police officer.
4 My two sisters are students.
5 My grandma works at a store.
6 My uncles work at a hospital.

39 **Play the Jobs game.**

at a	fire station
	hospital
	laboratory
	police station
	restaurant
	store
	college
on a	farm

Do I work at a hospital? No.

I Can

- talk about what people do and where they work.
- talk about creative jobs.
- find and use two subjects and two verbs.

unit 3 Working Hard!

1 Listen, look, and say.

1 make my bed

2 walk the dog

3 practice the piano

4 take out the trash

5 do the dishes

6 clean my room

7 study for a test

8 feed the fish

2 Listen, find, and say.

3 Play a game.

36 Unit 3 vocabulary (chores)

4 Listen and sing. What chores does Matt do?

Different Twins

My name's Matt,
And my name's Mike.
We want to talk to you.
I do my chores,
And I do, too.
But we are not alike.

**Mike and Matt, Matt and Mike.
These two twins are not alike.**

I'm Matt, I always clean my room.
I do my chores each day.
I sometimes do the dishes,
And then we go and play.

Chorus

I'm Mike, I always make my bed.
I do my chores each day.
I sometimes walk the dog,
And then we go and play.

Chorus

5 Use the chart to ask and answer questions about Matt.

Matt	Sun	Mon	Tue	Wed	Thu	Fri	Sat
clean his room	✓	✓	✓	✓	✓	✓	✓
feed the fish	✓	✓		✓		✓	✓
do the dishes	✓				✓		
take out the trash							

Does Matt clean his room?   Yes, he does.

THINK BIG Which of these are your favorite chores?
Why are chores important?

Story

 6 Listen and read. What time does Amy have to leave for school?

I Have a Lot to Do

1 Amy is thinking. Her mom comes into her bedroom.

2 Amy likes making lists. She often makes a list of things she has to do.

3 Amy has to do a lot of things before school.

4 Amy's clock still says 7:05.

5 What time does Amy have to leave? At 7:50? Oh, no!

6 Amy's never late for school. She doesn't want to be late today!

7 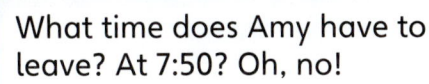 **Read and say true or false.**
1 Amy has to do a lot of things before school.
2 She has to eat breakfast.
3 She has to walk the dog.
4 She has to study for her English test.
5 She has to leave for school at 7:00.
6 She has to get a new alarm clock.

THINK BIG
What kinds of lists do people make?
How do lists help us remember things?
What other things help us remember?

Language in Action

8 Listen and look at the sentences. Help Luke and Amy make more.

[51]

study for a test   do the dishes   make my bed

take out the trash

What | do we | have to do | ?
We | have to | practice the piano | .
What | does she | have to do | ?
She | has to | walk the dog | .

9 Follow the lines. What do they have to do?

1
2
3

walk the dog
clean my room
do my homework
feed the fish

10 What about you? Ask and answer.

What do you have to do?

I have to practice the piano.

Language in Action

11 Listen to Alexia's week and find the three mistakes.

Monday	Tuesday	Wednesday	Thursday	Friday
do the dishes, practice the guitar	study for a test	take out the trash	make my bed	clean my room

12 Put the words in order. Then say.

1. sometimes | Do | make | your | bed? | you
2. do? | What | do | have | to | you
3. have | What | to | do? | Sally | does
4. never | the | dishes. | does | Jake
5. fish. | My | usually | feed | the | sisters

13 Look at the chart. Make sentences about Leo. Use always, usually, sometimes, and never.

| always *** | usually ** | sometimes * | never ✗ |

Leo's chores	Mon	Tue	Wed	Thu	Fri
study for a test	✓		✓		
clean his room	✓	✓	✓		✓
make his bed	✓	✓	✓	✓	✓
do the dishes					

language practice (adverbs of frequency) Unit 3

Content Connection | Math

 Do you get pocket money? What do you do when you want something expensive? Share with the class.

 Listen and read. Who can you work for?

> **CONTENT WORDS**
> adult   cash   clean   cost   earn
> let (someone) know   save   stranger   wash

Pocket Money

When you're a child, your parents take care of all your needs. You sometimes get a little pocket money to spend as you like, too. But when you want to buy something expensive, you need extra money. Where do you find it? You can't get a real job yet, but there are ways you can earn some extra cash.

Help with the housework Everyone has to help around the house. You probably have to clean your room and take out the trash. Do extra work to earn extra money. Ask your parents what extra things you can do for them and how much they can pay you for doing them.

Do chores for other people Sometimes other adult members of your family, friends, or neighbors are very busy, and they don't have time to do some chores. Let them know how you can help. Write what you can do and how much it costs on a piece of paper, make copies, and give them to the people you know.
Remember to be safe. Don't work for strangers. Always ask your parents and let them know where you are.

Save your money Save a little bit of the money you make every time. This way you always have extra cash!

To give you an idea of how much you can earn per week, look at Anne's chart:

	Amount	Number of times a week (x)	Subtotal
do the dishes	$1	3	$?
make breakfast	$2	2	$?
walk Mrs. Porter's dog	50 cents	6	$?
water Grandma's plants	$1	2	$?
wash Uncle Joe's car	$5	1	$?
			TOTAL: $

16 Look at 15. Read and say true or false.

1. Children can get a job to earn extra cash.
2. Everyone in the family has to do housework.
3. Parents pay their children for all the housework they do.
4. Some adults don't do their chores because they're busy.
5. Anne only works for family members.

17 Do the sums and complete Anne's chart in 15. Then ask and answer.

How much does Anne make from doing the dishes?

1 times 3 equals 3. She earns three dollars a week from doing the dishes.

THINK BIG Is it better to spend or save pocket money? Why? How much of your pocket money should you save?

PROJECT

18 Make a Chores chart to save money. Then present it to the class.

You want to buy a tablet. It costs $400.
First, make a chart with chores you can do and how often you can do them.
Calculate how much money you can make per week.
Calculate how many weeks until you have $400.

I earn 1 dollar each time I make my bed. I make my bed every day. 1 times 7 equals 7. I get 7 dollars a week. 10 times 7 equals 70. So for 10 weeks, I get 70 dollars!

My pocket money			
	Amount	Number of times	Subtotal
Make my bed	$1	7 times a week	$7 a week ($70 for 10 weeks)
Take out the trash			
Feed the cat			

content connection (pocket money) Unit 3 43

Grammar

 19 Look, listen, and point. Then say.

a

b

I hate cleaning up! I like studying in a messy bedroom. I hate studying in a clean bedroom!

I love cleaning up! I like studying in a clean bedroom. I hate studying in a messy bedroom!

I/We **like/love/hate cleaning** up.
You **like/love/hate getting** up early.
He/She/It **likes/loves/hates sleeping**.
They **like/love/hate watching** TV.

I/We **don't like/love/hate cleaning** up.
You **don't like/love/hate getting** up early.
He/She/It **doesn't like/love/hate sleeping**.
They **don't like/love/hate watching** TV.

Do I/we **like/love/hate cleaning** up?
Do you **like/love/hate getting** up early?
Does he/she/it **like/love/hate sleeping**?
Do they **like/love/hate watching** TV?

-ing
cook - cook**ing**
clean - clean**ing**
write - writ**ing**
shop - sho**pp**ing

20 Write the verbs in your notebook using -ing.

1 make ?
2 do ?
3 swim ?
4 feed ?
5 study ?
6 sit ?

Unit 3

Grammar

21 Read and complete. Use the correct form of the words from the box.

> cook   do   eat   get up   listen   swim

1 I don't like ? candy. It's bad for your teeth.
2 Why does Jerry hate ? sports?
3 We like ? . It's relaxing!
4 She loves ? to loud music.
5 Do you like ? in the ocean?
6 He doesn't like ? early in the morning.

22 Do the quiz. Are you a home person?

● love   ● like   ● don't like   ● hate

1 I ? cleaning my room.
2 I ? cleaning up the house.
3 I ? spending time at home.
4 I ? cooking with friends.
5 I ? washing dishes.
6 I ? having parties at my house.

Now find your score: love=4 points   like=3 points   don't like=2 points   hate=1 point

24–19   You love your home, and you're a great host! Your friends are lucky!
18–12   You like being at home, but you often have other things to do.
11–7   You let other people do all the work for you. Not nice!
6–1   Please don't invite me to your home!

23 Ask and answer. Use *like*, *love*, and *hate*. Write your partner's answers in your notebook.

1 watch horror movies?   ?
2 play sports?   ?
3 listen to classical music?   ?
4 read comic books?   ?
5 eat fast food?   ?
6 text?   ?

> Do you like watching horror movies?

> Yes, I do. I love watching horror movies.

> No, I don't like watching horror movies. I like watching comedies.

24 Use the information in 23 and write about your partner. Then share with the class.

? likes/doesn't like ?

grammar (*She loves sleeping. He hates cleaning up.*) Unit 3

Culture Connection | Around the World

Many Hands Make Light Work

1. Everyone knows that even difficult tasks can be easy to do if you have help. All around the world, families share their work at home but also the chores of the family business. Parents do most of them, but children help out when they can, too. Let's find out what chores these kids do.

2. Leah lives in Alaska. There's usually a lot of snow on the roads and the sidewalks. Everyone has to shovel snow to keep the entrance to their home clear. Leah shovels snow before she goes to school every day. Leah says, "I like shovelling snow!"

25 Discuss with a partner. Then check with your teacher.

What do you think the expression "Many hands make light work" means?
- **a** It means that when people work together, nothing goes right.
- **b** It means that when people work together, the work is easy.

Do you have an expression that means the same in your language?

26 Listen and read. Then match.

CONTENT WORDS
business entrance noodles
share shovel sidewalk
task tiring

1 Leah   a in France.
2 Ivan   lives   b in Singapore.
3 Chen Wei   c in Alaska.

27 Look at **26**. Answer the questions.

1 What does Leah do to help at home?
2 When does Leah do her chore?
3 What does Chin Wei's mother do?
4 Why does Chin Wei help his mother?
5 Who does Ivan help on his family's farm?
6 What time does Ivan get up every day?

3 Ivan lives on a goat farm in France. They get milk from their goats to make goat cheese and sell it. Ivan helps take care of the goats. Every morning, he has to get up at 5 o'clock. He helps his father feed the goats and get the milk. He goes to school after he does his chores. "I like helping my dad," he says.

4 Chen Wei's mother makes the best noodles, and people come to her restaurant from all over Singapore to eat them. The work can be very tiring for one person only, so after he does his homework, Chen Wei helps his mother cook noodles. "I love eating noodles, too!" he says.

It's great to help, isn't it?

28 Look at **26**. Play a game.

1. feed animals
2. help my mom cook
3. shovel the snow off our car
4. wash the empty bowls
5. wear warm gloves
6. help my father make cheese

 I have to feed animals.

 You're Ivan!

29 Ask your classmates what chores they have to do to help their family. Make a list. Look at this example:

What chores do you have to do to help your family?

Total number of people in class: 12
1. clean their room   10 out of 12
2. walk the dog   7 out of 12
3. ....

I clean my room.

 THINK BIG Which chores look difficult and which look easy? Why?

Writing | Paragraph: Titles

30 Find the words we **don't** capitalize in the titles.

> Use capital letters for most words in titles.
> Taking Care of a Big Dog

Good Things to Eat

My Brother and I

The Big Blue Car

A Day at the Park with Grandma

To the Moon and Back

31 Rewrite the titles. Use capital letters where necessary.

1. helping my dad
2. lots of chores for my brother
3. helping out around the house
4. a strange day out
5. the jobs I like
6. helping my family is fun
7. my sister's new job

32 How many English titles do you know? Write them with a partner.

ay, oy | Phonics

 33 **Listen, read, and repeat.**

1 ay   2 oy

 34 **Listen and find. Then say.**

M**ay**

t**oy**

 35 **Listen and blend the sounds.**

1 d-ay   day   2 j-oy   joy
3 s-ay   say   4 p-ay   pay
5 b-oy   boy   6 s-oy   soy
7 w-ay   way   8 r-ay   ray

 36 **Read aloud. Then listen and chant.**

What do we say?
It's May, it's May,
It's a nice day.
Come on, girls!
Come on, boys!
Bring your toys.

Values | Always be happy to help.

 37 Look and listen. Are they happy to help? Say **yes** or **no**.

1

2

3

 38 Role-play the dialogs in **37** with a partner.

PROJECT

39 Make a sock puppet. With a partner, use your puppet to role-play helping someone.

50 Unit 3 values

Review

40 Read and match. Then make statements for you. Use the words from the box.

> always   have to   never   sometimes   usually

1 study for
2 do
3 clean
4 walk the
5 practice

a dog
b the piano
c my room
d a test
e the dishes

41 Copy the chart in your notebook and complete for you. Then ask and answer.

My Chores	Sun	Mon	Tue	Wed	Thu	Fri	Sat
clean my room							
do my homework							
do the dishes							
study for a test							

Do you always clean your room?

No, I don't. I always do my homework.

42 Read and complete.

1 They don't like ❓ baseball. (play)
2 He loves ❓ people's pictures. (take)
3 She hates ❓ a bike. (ride)
4 You like ❓ juice. (drink)
5 I love ❓ in the ocean. (swim)

I Can

- talk about how often people do things.
- talk about what people like/don't like doing and have to do.
- talk about chores and pocket money.
- use capital letters in titles.

review/self-assessment Unit 3

Checkpoint | Units 1–3

How Well Do I Know It? Can I Use It?

1 Think about it. Read and draw. Practice.

😀 I know this.   😐 I need more practice.   😟 I don't know this.

#		PAGES			
1	**Daily activities:** eat breakfast, go to school, practice the piano…	4, 36	😀	😐	😟
2	**Telling time:** one o'clock, two thirty, 5:15…	5	😀	😐	😟
3	**Jobs:** cashier, firefighter, nurse…	20	😀	😐	😟
4	**Workplaces:** police station, restaurant, store…	21	😀	😐	😟
5	**When** does she get dressed? She gets dressed **at 7:00 in the morning**.	8	😀	😐	😟
6	What does he do **before** school? He eats breakfast **before** school. I watch TV **after** school.	9	😀	😐	😟
7	They **always/usually/sometimes/never** do their homework after school.	12, 41	😀	😐	😟
8	What **does** he **do**? He **is** a cashier. Where **does** he **work**? He **works** at a store.	24–25	😀	😐	😟
9	**Does** he **swim**? Yes, he **does**. I **play** music. I **don't do** sports.	28–29	😀	😐	😟
10	What **do** they **have to** do? They **have to** feed the fish.	40	😀	😐	😟
11	I/You/They **like/love/hate cleaning**. He/She/It **likes/loves/hates swimming**.	44–45	😀	😐	😟

I Can Do It!

2 **Get ready.**

A Complete the interview. Use the questions from the box. Then listen and check.

> Do you eat dinner at home?
> usually
> What do you do?
> What do you do before work?
> When do you go to work?
> Where do you work?

Katy: ¹ ?
Max: I'm a chef.
Katy: Oh, really? ² ?
Max: I work at a restaurant, the Pizza Palace.
Katy: I see. ³ ?
Max: I ⁴ ? go to work at 2:00. I come home at 11:00 at night.
Katy: OK. ⁵ ?
Max: I take a shower, eat breakfast, and get dressed. Then I feed my fish.
Katy: ⁶ ?
Max: No, I always eat dinner at the restaurant.

B Make more questions.
1. When ? ?
2. ? before work?
3. ? in the afternoon?

C Practice the dialog in **A** with a partner. Include your new questions.

Checkpoint Units 1–3   53

Checkpoint | Units 1–3

3 **Get set.**

 **STEP 1** Choose a job.

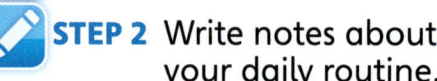 **STEP 2** Write notes about your daily routine.

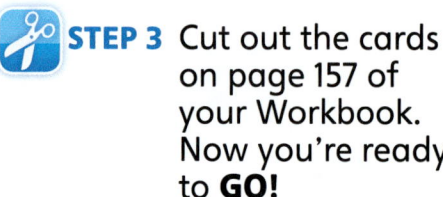 **STEP 3** Cut out the cards on page 157 of your Workbook. Now you're ready to **GO!**

4 **Go!**

A Use the cards to make questions. Interview your partner. Write about your partner's daily routine. Then switch roles.

B Work in groups. Tell your classmates about your partner's daily routine.

Luisa always eats breakfast before school.

5 Write about yourself in your notebook.

- When do you wake up?
- What do you like doing after school?
- What do you do before school?
- What time do you go to bed?
- What chores do you have to do?
- What chores do you never do?

How Well Do I Know It Now?

6 Think about it. Look at page 52 and your notebook. Draw again.

A Use a different color.

B Read and think.
I can start the next unit.
I can ask my teacher for help and then start the next unit.
I can practice and then start the next unit.

7 Rate this Checkpoint.

very easy   easy   hard   very hard   fun   OK   not fun

Checkpoint Units 1–3

Units 1–3 Exam Preparation

– Part A –

Listen and write. There is one example.

My dad's farm

Name of farm: _____Happy Farm_____

1 **Where?** near the _____

2 **How many chickens:** _____

3 **Color of cow:** _____

4 **Dog's name:** _____

5 **What time starts work?** _____ in the morning

56 Listening part 2

– Part B –

Read the story. Choose a word from the box. Write the correct word next to numbers 1–6. There is one example.

My name is Charlie. My mom and dad are _____nurses_____. They work at the (1) _____. They usually work in the morning, but sometimes they start work in the evening. They have to wear a white uniform.

When my (2) _____ work in the evening, my grandma and grandpa come to our house. I play video (3) _____ with my grandpa. He's very good! My grandma always makes dinner, and I take out the (4) _____. Then we (5) _____ TV for an hour, and I go to my room. In the morning, my grandma always tells me, "Make your (6) _____ before you go!"

Example

nurses   games   restaurant   parents   bed

play   watch   hospital   trash

(7) Now choose the best name for the story.

Check (✓) one box.

Charlie's video games ☐

My mom is a nurse ☐

Grandparents always help ☐

Reading and Writing part 4   57

unit 4 Amazing Animals

 1 Listen, look, and say.

1 bear
2 deer
3 owl
4 camel
5 lizard
6 penguin
7 toucan
8 sea lion
9 shark

 2 Listen, find, and say.

 3 Play a game.

58 Unit 4 vocabulary (animals)

4 Listen and sing. How many birds are in the song?

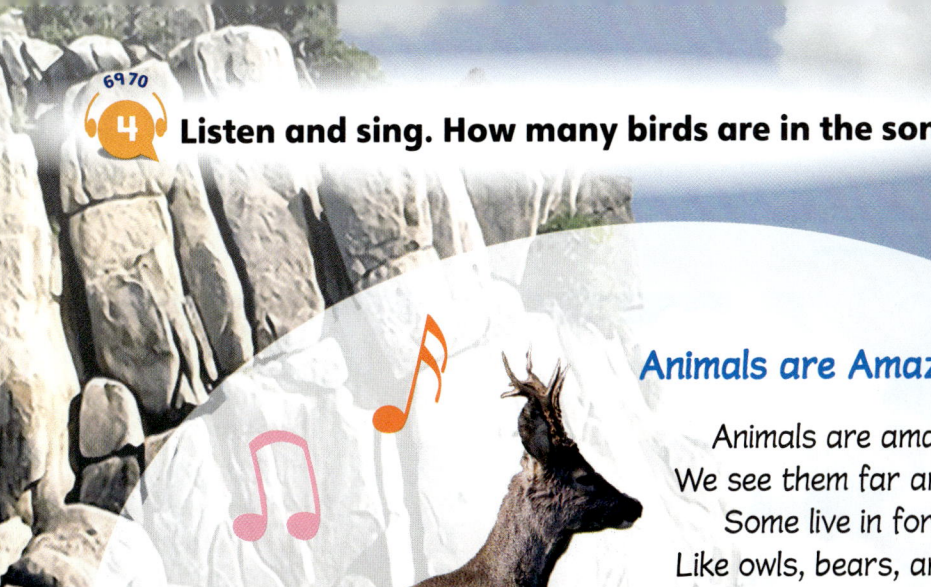

Animals are Amazing!

Animals are amazing!
We see them far and near.
Some live in forests
Like owls, bears, and deer.

Some live in deserts
Like camels and some snakes.
Some live in water,
In oceans, seas, and lakes.

Amazing, amazing animals
What can animals do?
They can fly, they can swim, they can jump!
We share the earth with you!

5 Match the animals to places. Ask and answer.

> deserts   forests   ice and snow   jungles
> lakes   mountains   oceans   rain forests

Where do lizards live?

Some live in deserts and some in lakes.

THINK BIG Look at the pictures. Which is your favorite animal and why?

Story

6 Listen and read. Can Smartie talk?

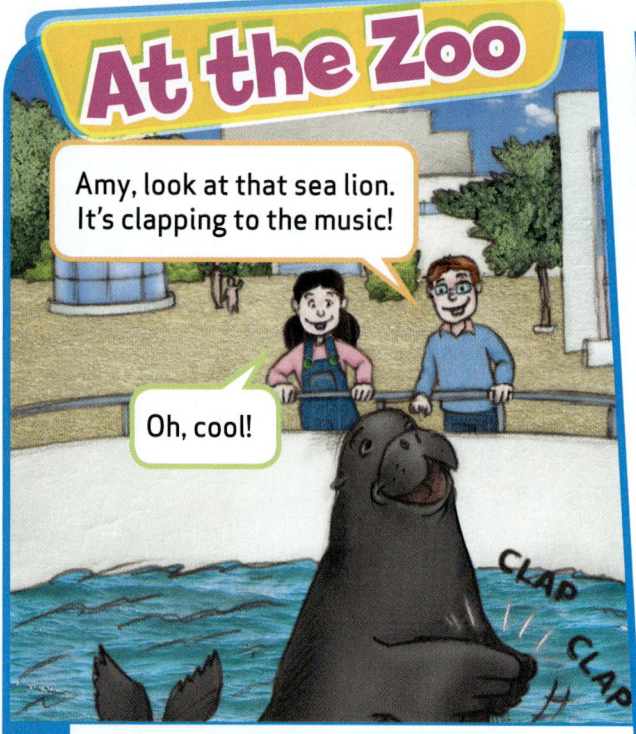

1. Luke and Amy are watching a sea lion show at the zoo.

2. Luke has to cover his ears.

3. The sea lion can balance a ball on its nose!

4. Then Luke and Amy watch a parrot show.

5 The parrot's name is Smartie.

6 When Smartie starts talking, Smartie can't stop!

7 Read and match. Make sentences.

1 Sea lions can't
2 Sea lions can
3 Smartie is a
4 Smartie can
5 Smartie can't

a stop talking.
b parrot.
c say its name.
d sing very well.
e do great tricks.

THINK BIG What other animals are very smart?
What can they do?
What different ways are there to learn about animals in a zoo?

Language in Action

8 Listen and look at the sentences. Help Luke and Amy make more.

[climb trees] [swim] [run]
[camels] [lizards] [toucans]

[What] [can] [parrots] [do] [?]
[Parrots] [can] [talk and fly] [.]
[What] [can] [you] [do] [?]
[I] [can] [talk but] [I] [can't] [fly] [?]

9 Make the questions with *can*. Then answer with a partner.
1 What/kangaroos/do?
2 What/monkeys/do?
3 What/deer/do?
4 What/crocodiles/do?
5 What/you/do?

10 Make statements. Then say *true* or *false*.

Elephants can run and fly.

False! Elephants can run but they can't fly.

Unit 4 language practice (*What can bears do?*)

Language in Action

11 Copy the chart and complete. Listen and check. Then complete for you.

	swim	fly	climb trees	run	?
bears					
camels					
sharks					
lizards					
?					

12 Look at **11**. Ask and answer.

13 Read the dialog. What are the two animals? Now role-play with a partner.

A: Are you ready for an animal quiz?
B: Yes, I am!
A: OK. These animals live in ice and snow. They can swim, but they can't fly.
B: I know. ¹ ?
A: Right! Now it's your turn.
B: OK. They live in forests. They can climb trees and swim.
A: Snakes?
B: No. They have four legs and can run fast.
A: Oh, I know. ² ?
B: That's right!

language practice (*can/can't*) Unit 4

Content Connection | Science

14 Discuss in groups.

What's the best way for wild animals not to be eaten by other animals?
a Hide.   b Make a lot of noise.   c Sleep in the open.

15 Listen, read, and match pictures **a–d** to paragraphs **1–4**. Then check your answer in **14**.

> **CONTENT WORDS**
> blend in   bottom of the ocean   desert   rain forest
> stone   surroundings   tree bark

Animal Camouflage

a

Many animals blend in with their surroundings. This is called camouflage. Camouflage helps animals in different ways. Some use it to find food, but others use it because they don't want to become food! Animals use color, body shape, or both to blend in. If they do this well, other animals can't see them.

1 Polar Bears Hide in the Snow

Polar bears, for example, are found in the ice and snow. Everything around them is white. They're covered in white fur, but their eyes, noses, and the bottoms of their feet are black. When they hunt for food, they sometimes cover their eyes and nose with their paws. Because everything around them is white, it isn't easy to see a polar bear in the snow.

2 Smart Chameleons Change Color

But what happens when the surroundings have different colors? Meet the chameleons, masters of camouflage. Chameleons are found in rain forests and in deserts. These smart animals can change their color to match their surroundings. On a brown rock in the desert, they can be brown. In a green tree in the rain forest, they can be green. Genius!

b

3 Not a Stone, But a Stonefish

Stonefish use camouflage to get food. They look like stones on the bottom of the ocean. The fish they eat can't see them. If a fish touches a stonefish by mistake, it stings them to death and eats them.

4 Gray Tree Frogs Can't Be Seen

d

Gray tree frogs, however, use camouflage to hide. They're found in the forests of North America. Because they live in trees, they look like a tree branch. The birds and snakes that eat gray tree frogs can't see them against the bark of the tree.

c

THINK BIG Do you know any other animals that use camouflage? Where do they live? What do they look like? How do they blend in?

16 Look at **15**. Read and match.

1 Camouflage helps animals
2 Polar bears are covered in white fur to
3 Chameleons can
4 Stonefish wait for their food to
5 Gray tree frogs
6 Birds and snakes

a come to them.
b live in forests.
c blend in with the snow.
d hide from other animals.
e hunt for tree frogs.
f change their color.

17 Complete the fact cards.

PROJECT

18 Make four cards like the ones in **17**. Write about the animals in the list or use your own ideas. Then play a game.

snowy owls
stick insects
octopus
leopards

It's found in trees. It looks like a small branch of a tree.

It's a stick insect!

Good job! You get one point.

Grammar

19 Look, listen, and read. Are they hungry?

Dog: Woof! Our humans are having a party!
Cat: Shhh! Walk quietly!
Dog: Look at those burgers! Can we eat them?
Cat: OK, but can you run fast?

quiet	quietly
slow	slowly
easy	easily
careful	carefully

	But…
good	well
fast	fast
hard	hard
far	far

She works very **hard**.
Can he run **fast**?
I don't feel **well**.

20 Read, match, and complete.

1 Amanda is slow.
2 You are a fast eater.
3 David is loud.
4 Fred is a good artist.
5 My mom's a careful driver.
6 I'm a bad cook.

a She drives ?.
b He can paint very ?.
c You eat ?.
d She walks ?.
e I cook ?.
f He speaks ?.

21 Read and complete. Use the words from the box.

> carefully   easily   far   fast   hard   well

1 I work very ? at school.
2 Big cats can run very ?.
3 Don't push the door. It opens ?.
4 Please cross the road ?.
5 I know him very ?. He's my best friend.
6 We don't have to walk ?. The house is over there.

66 Unit 4

Grammar

22 Look at the chart. Read and make a list in your notebook.

1 Adnan is a quiet child.
2 She's playing very badly today.
3 I have to study hard for this test.
4 It's a very good movie.
5 You're walking very fast!
6 You have to be careful at work.

quiet	badly

23 Read and choose.

1 I can read Italian, but I can't speak very **good/well** yet.
2 This place is very **noisy/noisily**!
3 Eat your food **slow/slowly**.
4 You have to speak **quiet/quietly** in the library.
5 Let's finish **quick/quickly**! We don't have time.
6 The music isn't very **loud/loudly**.

24 Read and complete for you.

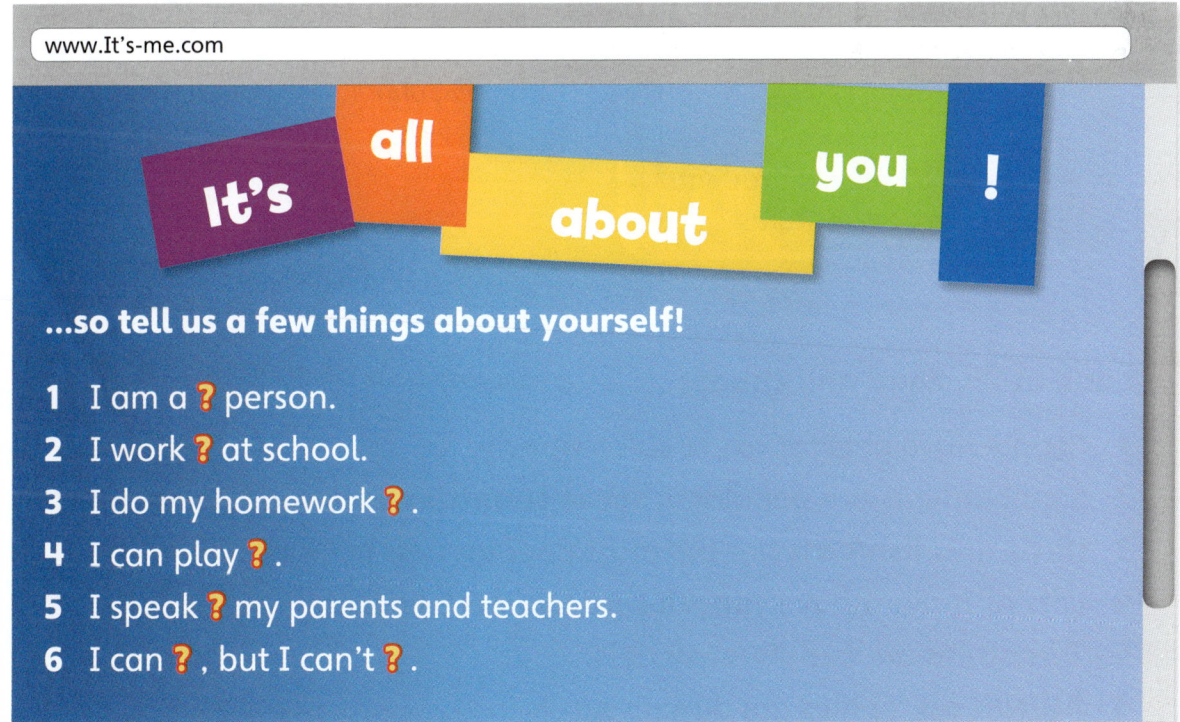

www.It's-me.com

It's all about you!

...so tell us a few things about yourself!

1 I am a ? person.
2 I work ? at school.
3 I do my homework ? .
4 I can play ? .
5 I speak ? my parents and teachers.
6 I can ? , but I can't ? .

grammar (*It's a slow car. It moves slowly.*) Unit 4

Culture Connection | Around the World

Pets in Different Places

1   Many people around the world have pets. Pets are good company, but they also help us in other ways. We get exercise when we take our dogs for a walk. They also keep us safe. Cats keep mice and big insects away from our homes. Our pets help us relax, and we love playing with them or just watching them!

2   There are lots of different pets around the world. Every country has its favorites, but cats, dogs, birds, fish, and small rodents are popular almost everywhere. In the United States, there are about 93 million pet cats. Cats are very popular in China, too. The Chinese believe that they bring good luck to a home. Birds and goldfish are also popular. In fact, they're the top two favorite pets in China. Birds such as the colorful parakeet are popular in Mexico. Parakeets like playing with people, and they can talk! In Italy, lots of people have canaries. Canaries can sing all day!

25 Why do you think people have animals as pets? Make a list of reasons as a class.

26 Listen and read. Check your answers in **25**. Then complete the chart.

CONTENT WORDS
alligators   canaries   geckos
goldfish   parakeets   rodents
snakes   tarantulas

Popular pets	Unusual pets	Dangerous pets
?	?	?

27 Look at **26**. Read and choose.

1 People have pets for **exercise/company**.
2 Small rodents are popular in **some countries only/many countries**.
3 **Birds and fish/Cats** are the most popular pets in China.
4 Lots of Italians have **canaries/parakeets** as pets.
5 Tarantulas are **cuddly/easy** pets.
6 **All/Not all** reptiles are dangerous.

3   One of Japan's popular pets is the bunny rabbit. There are even bunny cafés where you can have coffee and spend time with these furry animals or buy one!

4   Some people choose unusual or exotic pets. Chilean Rose Hair Tarantulas are quiet and easy to keep, but they aren't very cuddly. They don't usually bite, but if they do, it can be painful! There are millions of reptile pet owners around the world. Reptiles such as iguanas or geckos aren't dangerous, but snakes or alligators can be very dangerous, so pet owners need to be extra careful.

5   There's a type of pet for everyone. People all over the world choose different pets for different reasons. One thing is important, though. Our pets are our friends, and they need our love and care.

28 **Work with a partner. Discuss which pet is best for each person.**

Ethan
- is often away from home
- lives in a very small apartment

Isabella
- wants a colorful pet
- loves talking to animals

Jed
- is allergic to animal fur
- wants an unusual pet

Sandra
- lives in a big apartment
- likes staying at home

How about a hamster for Ethan?

I don't think so. He's often away from home. Hamsters need feeding every day.

THINK BIG Some people have wild animals as pets. Do you agree?

Writing | Paragraph: Topic Sentences

29 Listen and read. What's Spotty like?

title →

topic sentence →

My Favorite Pet
by Aaron Michaels

My favorite pet is my snake, Spotty. He is a corn snake. He is 50 centimeters long, and he is red and white. I feed him one small mouse every week. He is friendly. He does not bite people. Some people don't like snakes, but snakes can make good pets.

30 Read 26 again. Find the first topic sentence.

> A topic sentence gives the main idea in a paragraph.

31 Read and match the titles to the topic sentences.

Title	Topic Sentence
1 A Day at the Zoo	a My sister and I have many pets at home.
2 My Mother's Job	b My favorite time of day at school is art class.
3 My Favorite Class	c I have to do lots of chores at home after school.
4 After-School Jobs	d My mother is a chef at an Italian restaurant.
5 Our Pets	e When I go to the zoo, I spend the whole day there.

32 What is your favorite animal? Write a title and a topic sentence.

ea, oi, oe | Phonics

33 **Listen, read, and repeat.**

1 ea   2 oi   3 oe

34 **Listen and find. Then say.**

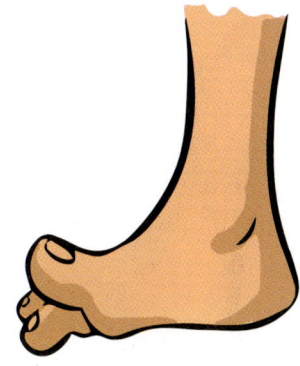

eat   coin   toe

35 **Listen and blend the sounds.**

1 s-ea   sea   2 b-oi-l   boil
3 b-ea-n bean   4 t-ea   tea
5 p-ea-ch peach   6 m-ea-t   meat
7 oi-l   oil   8 f-oe   foe

36 **Read aloud. Then listen and chant.**

So, Joe, boil the beans,
Add the oil,
Add the meat.
Eat the beans,
Eat the meat,
Eat the peach,
And drink the tea.

Values | **Protect animals and their habitats.**

37 Look at the map of animals in Australia. Play a game.

Animals of Australia

- parrot (rain forest)
- kangaroo (desert)
- dingo (grasslands)
- koala (forest)
- kookaburra (forest)

> Parrots in Australia live in the desert.

> Wrong! They live in rain forests.

PROJECT

38 Work in a group. Make an **Animals Map**.

- Choose a continent.
- Research the animals that live there.
- Draw and label your part of the map.

bear (forest)

penguin (ice and snow)

mountain lion (mountains)

parrot (rain forest)

snake (rain forest)

lizard (rain forest)

Review

39 Complete the sentences. Use the correct form of the words from the box.

> bad   careful   easy   good   hard   slow

1 Turtles walk very ?.
2 He always studies very ?.
3 Watch out! You should play ?.
4 The choir is great. They sing ?.
5 Sorry, I can't help you. I draw really ?.
6 I did great! I answered all the questions ?.

40 Complete the dialog. Then ask and answer.

Daniel: Where do sharks live?
Teresa: ¹ ?.
Daniel: Right. ² ?
Teresa: Camels live in the desert.
Daniel: Right again! ³ ?
Teresa: Camels can walk and run a little, but they can't jump or fly.
Daniel: How about penguins? Can they swim and fly?
Teresa: ⁴ ?
Daniel: That's right!

41 Make sentences about toucans and sea lions.
What can they do?
What can't they do?
Where are they found?

I Can

- talk about what animals can/can't do and where they're found.
- find and use adverbs.
- find and use topic sentences.

unit 5 Wonderful Weather!

1 Listen, look, and say.

1 It's windy.

2 It's cold and snowy.

The Weather today

hot
warm
cool
cold

3 It's cool and cloudy.

4 It's hot and sunny.

5 It's warm and rainy.

2 Listen, find, and say.

3 Play a game.

4 Listen and sing. What's the weather like today?

Cool Weekend!

What's the weather like today?
Rainy, sunny, hot, or cold?

On Sunday, it was rainy,
It was very cold, too.
I was nice and warm in my winter coat,
Outside the sky wasn't blue!

Now it's Monday. It's sunny.
Great! I can go out and play.
Oh, no! I have to go to school.
Never mind! The weekend was cool!

Chorus (x2)

5 Listen and find. Then ask and answer for you.

a — sunglasses, sandals, shorts

b — sweater, scarf

What do you wear on sunny days?

On sunny days, I wear shorts, a T-shirt, and sunglasses.

c — raincoat

d — coat

THINK BIG What weather is good for...
a soccer practice?
b a walk in the park?
c going to the beach?
d going skiing?

song/vocabulary (clothes) Unit 5

Story

 6 Listen and read. Where is Amy going today?

1. Amy is happy. Today her class is going on a hike.

2. Mom doesn't think Amy is ready.

3. Mom doesn't want Amy to get wet.

4. She doesn't want Amy to get cold.

5 Amy isn't worried about the weather.

6 Amy is ready for all kinds of weather!

7 Look at the story. Answer the questions with a partner.
1 What's Amy's class doing today?
2 What was the weather like yesterday?
3 What was the weather like last night?
4 What's the weather like today?
5 What's Amy wearing at the end of the story?

THINK BIG Do you think it's a good idea for Amy to take so many clothes?
What clothes would you take?

Language in Action

8 Listen and look at the sentences. Help Luke and Amy make more.

cold | windy | cloudy

What is the weather like today?
It's warm and sunny now.
What was the weather like yesterday?
It was rainy and cold.
I wasn't hot.
We weren't warm last Sunday.

9 Look at the weather chart. Answer the questions.

M	T	W	Th	F
 snowy	 rainy	 cloudy	 windy	 sunny

1. Today is Monday. What's the weather like today?
2. Today is Tuesday. What's the weather like today?
3. It's sunny. What day is it today?
4. It's windy. What day is it today?
5. Today is Thursday. What was the weather like yesterday?

10 Ask and answer.

I'm wearing a T-shirt, shorts, and sandals. What's the weather like?

It's sunny and warm.

78 Unit 5 language practice (*What's the weather like today? What was the weather like yesterday?*)

Language in Action

11 Read and find the correct sentence and say. Correct for you.

1. It is sunny yesterday.
   It was sunny yesterday.
2. Today it's snowy.
   Yesterday it's snowy.
3. It's cool and windy now.
   It was cool and windy now.
4. It was rainy last night.
   It is rainy last night.
5. We aren't warm last Sunday.
   We weren't warm last Sunday.
6. She isn't cold today.
   She wasn't cold today.

It wasn't sunny yesterday.

12 Complete the roleplay with **is** or **was**. Then say with your partner.

Derya: My vacation is a lot of fun. Yesterday, ¹ ❓ great! I ² ❓ at the beach all day!

George: Wow! What ³ ❓ the weather like yesterday?

Derya: It ⁴ ❓ hot and sunny. What ⁵ ❓ the weather like at home today?

George: It ⁶ ❓ cool and rainy.

13 Put the temperatures in order. Start with cold. Make sentences about what you are wearing.

cold   cool   hot   warm

It's cold today. I'm wearing boots, pants, a sweater, coat, and gloves.

Content Connection | Geography

14 What's your favorite type of weather? Discuss as a class.

15 Listen and read. Then match.

CONTENT WORDS
average   climate   degrees Celsius
desert   dry   extreme   mild   minus

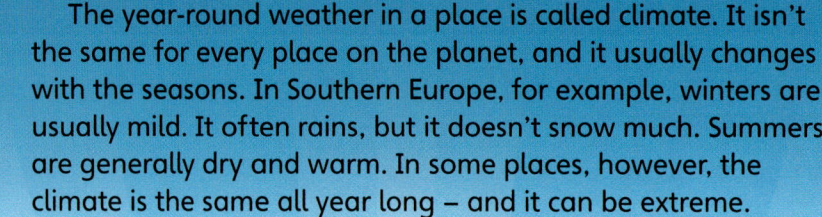

Changing Climates

1 The year-round weather in a place is called climate. It isn't the same for every place on the planet, and it usually changes with the seasons. In Southern Europe, for example, winters are usually mild. It often rains, but it doesn't snow much. Summers are generally dry and warm. In some places, however, the climate is the same all year long – and it can be extreme.

2 The Lut Desert in Iran is very hot and dry all year round. The temperatures there can be 70 degrees Celsius! Because of the extreme temperatures, some parts of the Lut desert have no life at all. Now you know why not many people go there! The Atacama Desert in Chile, on the other hand, is very popular with tourists. The temperatures are mild all year round, but in some parts of this desert, it never rains at all. People say the Atacama Desert looks like the moon, and they love its natural beauty.

3 If it never rains in the Atacama Desert, it rains almost every day in Lloró, Colombia. Lloró gets an average of 13 meters of rain every year. That's a lot! The trees grow very quickly because of the wet climate.

4 In Oymyakon, Russia, winters are very long and cold. It snows all the time, and temperatures can be minus 70 degrees Celsius. If you think that snow means no school, you're wrong. Schools close only when the temperature is below minus 52 degrees Celsius!

5 Places with a good climate are very popular. But a lot of sun and high temperatures isn't everyone's idea of a good climate. Some people really like the cold or wet weather. So long as everyone's happy!

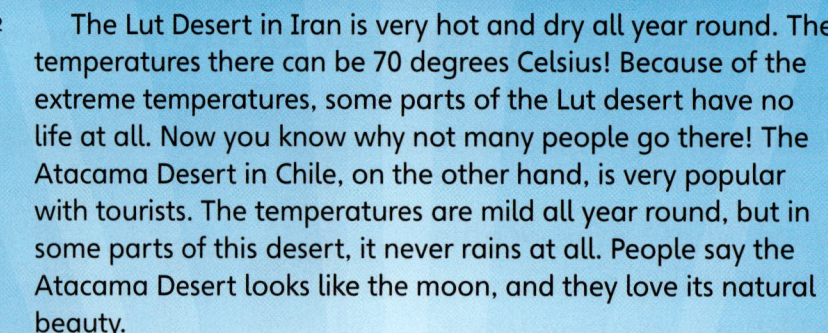

1 Southern Europe   a No rain.
2 Lut Desert, Iran   b Extreme cold.
3 Atacama Desert, Chile   c Lots of rain.
4 Lloró, Colombia   d Mild winters.
5 Oymyakon, Russia   e Very hot and dry.

 **THINK BIG** What difficulties do people who live in extreme climates have?

16 Look at **15**. Correct the mistakes.
1. The whole planet has the same climate.
2. It usually snows in Southern Europe in winter.
3. There's no life in the Lut Desert at all.
4. The Atacama Desert doesn't have many visitors.
5. Lloró and the Atacama Desert have the same climate.
6. Schools in Oymyakon close only when it's below minus 70 degrees Celsius.

17 Complete the chart with information about the climate where you live. Use the chart to ask and answer with a partner.

Place	Climate	Weather	Effect
desert	hot and dry	never rains	not many plants grow there
rain forest	hot and wet	rains all the time	there are lots of plants and trees
high mountains	cold and snowy	snows a lot	they're great places for skiing
?	?	?	?

 What's the weather like in the desert?

It's hot and dry. It never rains in the desert. That's why not many plants grow there.

PROJECT

18 Choose one of the places in the list and make a **Climate** poster. Then present it to the class.

The Amazon Rain Forest
The Sahara Desert
The Mediterranean
The Andean Mountain Range

The Canadian Arctic is very cold and snowy. In the winter, temperatures can be minus 50 degrees Celsius. As a result, many animals sleep all winter.

Grammar

19 Look and read. Then say.

a   b

What was your vacation like? Was it hot and sunny? The weather was great here!

It wasn't sunny, and it wasn't hot. It was rainy, and it was miserable. There wasn't a nice beach, and there wasn't a swimming pool.

Oh! Were there nice stores?

Yes, there were fantastic stores but they weren't open!

I/He/She/It		**was**	late.
You/We/They		**were**	early.
I/He/She/It		**wasn't**	in the desert.
You/We/They		**weren't**	freezing.
Was	I/he/she/it	thirsty?	Yes, I/he/she/it **was**. No, I/he/she/it **wasn't**.
Were	you/we/they	hungry?	Yes, you/we/they **were**. Yes, you/we/they **weren't**.

There **was**	a turtle in the zoo.
Was **there**	any water?
There **wasn't**	cake on the table.
There **were**	umbrellas on the chair.

20 Read and choose.

1 Albert Einstein **was/were** from Germany.
2 Michael Jackson **was/were** a singer.
3 There **was/were** ice on the River Thames last winter.
4 There **was/were** seven dwarfs in the fairytale *Snow White*.
5 The Olympic Games **was/were** in London in 2012.
6 The first people on the moon **was/were** American.

Grammar

21 **Make true sentences for you. Use was/wasn't or were/weren't.**

1. It ? Sunday yesterday.
2. We ? at the beach on Saturday.
3. I ? hungry at 9 o' clock.
4. My friends ? at my house yesterday.
5. The weather ? bad yesterday.
6. Our dinner ? yummy yesterday.

22 **Put the words in order. Then say.**

1. with your family | you | last weekend? | Were
2. were | Where | night? | last | you
3. you | fifteen | Were | on your last birthday?
4. hot | it | Was | a | yesterday? | day
5. Was | a movie | on TV | there | last night?
6. Were | your | and raincoat | umbrella | bag | in your | yesterday?

23 **Think about two things from the past or choose from the list. Discuss with a partner.**

- your last school (teacher, classroom, students, playground, friends, lessons)
- the weather last summer (rainy, sunny, cold, hot, windy)
- your town a hundred years ago (stores, big/small, people, houses, parks)

My last school was nice. There were three teachers, and the classroom was big. There were twenty students. There was a cool playground. Our classes were easy. My friends were Katie, Adam, and Jamie.

grammar (*Were they hungry? Yes, they were.*) Unit 5

Culture Connection | Around the World

All Weather Fun

Children around the world enjoy outdoor sports and activities. In the United States, many children play baseball. In India and England, cricket and field hockey are popular. And, of course, children all over the world play soccer. But when the weather is bad, it isn't much fun to play any of these sports. So what can you do? Wear the right clothes and make the weather work for you. Here are some ideas.

1

If it's too windy, it can be difficult to play soccer or other outdoor ball sports. But a windy day is great for flying a kite. Children all over the world enjoy flying kites, but it's a very popular activity in Japan and other Asian countries. It's even more fun if you make the kite yourself. It's very easy, and you can find all the information on the Internet!

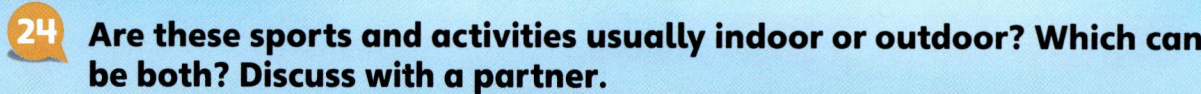

24 Are these sports and activities usually indoor or outdoor? Which can be both? Discuss with a partner.

soccer   basketball   bowling   skateboarding   Ping-Pong
skiing   volleyball   field hockey   baseball   swimming

25 Listen and read. Match the titles (A–C) to paragraphs 1–3.

> **CONTENT WORDS**
> cricket   fill up   kite
> sledding   snowball fight

A No umbrellas, please!
B Put on your wool hats and gloves!
C Hold on tightly!

26 Look at **25**. Read and say **true** or **false**.

1 Baseball is very popular in India.
2 You can't play all outdoor sports on windy days.
3 It's easy to make a kite.
4 In parts of Africa, it rains year-round.
5 You can ride a sled with or without a dog.
6 Pulling a sled isn't fun for dogs.

84 Unit 5

2 ❓

Rain doesn't stop African children from having fun. In parts of Africa, it's dry for many months of the year. But when the rain comes, the dry rivers and lakes fill up quickly. Kids love it. They go swimming and play games in the water. It's a fun time for everyone when it rains.

3 ❓

Having fun in the snow is easy. Everyone loves snowball fights and building snowmen. In Alaska and parts of Canada, where it snows a lot, kids often go sledding. Some kids also do an interesting sport called dog sledding. Dogs pull the sled and the kids ride on it. The dogs and the kids love it!

So next time the weather is bad, don't stay in and watch TV. Even if it's windy, wet, or cold, there are lots of fun things to do outside.

27 Ask and answer with a partner.

skiing	between -1 and -6 degrees Celsius, clear sky
wind surfing	windy, sunny, or cloudy
soccer	any kind of weather except extreme weather
ocean swimming	hot, sunny
rock climbing	warm, not very windy

What's the best weather for skiing?

When the temperature is between -1 and -6 degrees Celsius and the sky is clear.

THINK BIG How many outdoor sports and activities can you think of? Make a list.

Writing | Paragraph: Detail Sentences

28 Read. Then choose.

> Here is a topic sentence.
>
> *My favorite season is summer.*
>
> After the topic sentence, we give more information with detail sentences.
>
> *In the summer where I live, the weather is usually sunny and hot. I like going to the beach with my friends. We swim or play volleyball.*

`detail sentence   topic sentence`

1 A ❓ tells us what the paragraph is about.
2 A ❓ gives us more information.

29 Read the topic sentence below. Which sentences give details about this topic?

Topic sentence: *Winter is my favorite time of year.*

1 We like building snowmen in the winter, too.
2 It's not cold in the summer.
3 My friends and I like to go sledding.
4 We usually wear hats and gloves in the winter.
5 My sister's favorite season is spring.
6 It's cold and snowy in the winter, but I like it.

Writing Steps

30 Write about your favorite season.

1 Choose your favorite season.
2 Write a title.
3 Write a topic sentence.
4 Write three detail sentences.

sc, sw, sn, sl | Phonics

31 Listen, read, and repeat.

1 **sc**　　2 **sw**　　3 **sn**　　4 **sl**

32 Listen and find. Then say.

scarf　　**sw**eet　　**sn**ail　　**sl**eep

33 Listen and blend the sounds.

1　s-c-ou-t　scout　　2　s-n-a-ck　snack
3　s-w-i-m　swim　　4　s-l-i-m　slim
5　s-n-ow　snow　　6　s-w-a-n　swan
7　s-l-ow　slow　　8　s-c-ar　scar

34 Read aloud. Then listen and chant.

A slow snail is eating a snack,
And a slim swan is swimming.

phonics (sc, sw, sn, sl) Unit 5

Values | Prepare for the weather.

35 Look, listen, and point.

a

b

c

PROJECT

36 Work with a group. Make a **Prepare for the Weather** checklist.

Prepare for the Weather

- sunscreen ☐
- gloves ☐
- sunglasses ☐
- hat ☐
- water ☐
- umbrella ☐

Review

37 Look at the weather reports. Complete the questions and answers.

Barcelona, Spain	
Yesterday	Today
☀️ 🍃	🌧️
Temperature: 33 °C	Temperature: 28 °C

Glasgow, Scotland	
Yesterday	Today
🌨️	☁️
Temperature: 4 °C	Temperature: 12 °C

1 What/weather/Barcelona/yesterday?
2 Yesterday, in Barcelona it was ❓.
3 What/weather/Barcelona/today?
4 Today, it's ❓.
5 What/weather/Glasgow/yesterday?
6 ❓
7 What/weather/Glasgow/today?
8 ❓

38 Find the differences. Talk with a partner.

Picture 1

Picture 2

In Picture 1, it's hot and sunny.

In Picture 2, it's cold and snowy.

39 Choose one picture from **38**. Write a topic sentence and three detail sentences.

I Can
- talk about the weather today and in the past.
- talk about clothes.
- talk about climates around the world.
- find and use detail sentences.

unit 6 Smells Good!

1 Listen, look, and say.

Senses

1 This music sounds beautiful.

2 This band sounds awful.

3 This soup tastes horrible.

4 This pie tastes delicious.

5 This apple tastes sweet.

6 These flowers smell nice.

7 My hair looks terrible.

8 My sweater feels soft.

9 These shoes feel tight.

2 Listen, find, and say.   **3** Play a game.

4 Listen and sing. Where do the girls like going?

Grandma's House

We love my Grandma's house.
It always smells so nice.
It smells like ginger cookies
Sweet, with a little spice!

**Yummy smells and her smiling face.
We really love my Grandma's place.**

Grandma likes playing old songs
From when she was very young.
The music sounds so wonderful,
We have to sing along.

We always do my favorite thing
Baking ginger cookies.
They taste so nice and yummy,
We are both very lucky!

Chorus

5 Match the pictures to the words. Then ask and answer about 1.

 1
 2
 3
 4
 5

feel
look
smell
sound
taste

 This pie tastes delicious.

Number 4.

THINK BIG Can you think of other things you describe with these adjectives?
sweet   tight   beautiful   horrible

Story

 6 Listen and read. What kind of soup does Luke try?

1 Luke smells something bad coming from the kitchen.

2 It *is* fish soup. Luke thinks it smells horrible.

3 Amy tries the soup.

4 Luke tries the soup.

5   Luke thinks the soup tastes awful.

6   Amy has a cold. That's why she can't taste the soup.

7   Put the sentences in order.
- a   Amy thinks the soup tastes OK.
- b   Luke thinks the soup tastes terrible.
- c   Luke thinks the fish soup smells awful.
- d   Amy tries the soup.
- e   Luke tries the soup.
- f   Luke asks Amy to try the soup.

THINK BIG   Which senses do we use when we are…
- a   in a restaurant?
- b   at a soccer game?
- c   at school?

How do our senses make us aware of danger?

Language in Action

8 🎧 112 **Listen and look at the sentences. Help Luke and Amy make more.**

sound · look · smell

horrible · OK · nice

How does the soup taste?
It tastes delicious.
How do the sandals feel?
They feel tight.

9 🎧 113 **Are the adjectives positive or negative? Copy and complete. Then listen and check.**

amazing · awful · bad · beautiful · delicious · good · horrible · nice · terrible

Positive	Negative
amazing	awful

94 Unit 6 language practice (*It feels soft./They taste delicious.*)

Language in Action

10 Read and choose. Complete the answers.

> awful   good   great   nice   soft

1 A: How do these flowers **smell/smells**?
   B: ❓.
2 A: How does my new shirt **look/looks**?
   B: ❓. I like the color.
3 A: How does the sandwich **taste/tastes**?
   B: ❓. I don't like tomatoes!
4 A: How does the school band **sound/sounds**?
   B: ❓. They practice every day.
5 A: How do your new gloves **feel/feels**?
   B: ❓.

11 Complete the questions.

1 ❓ the guitar music sound?
2 ❓ the flowers smell?
3 ❓ my hair look today?
4 ❓ that pizza taste?
5 ❓ the shoes feel?

12 Ask and answer. Use the words in the boxes.

> beautiful   delicious   great   horrible   soft   tight

> apples   flowers   hat   music   pants

How does the music sound?

It sounds beautiful.

language practice (*How do they taste? They taste great.*) Unit 6

Content Connection | Science

13 Discuss with a partner.

1. How many senses do you think we have: 4, 5, or 6?
2. What sense do we use these parts of the body for?
   a fingers   b nose   c eyes   d ears   e tongue   f feet   g brain

14 Listen and read. Then check your answers in **13**.

> **CONTENT WORDS**
> avoid   brain   danger   echo   information
> senses   sound waves   taste buds   tongue

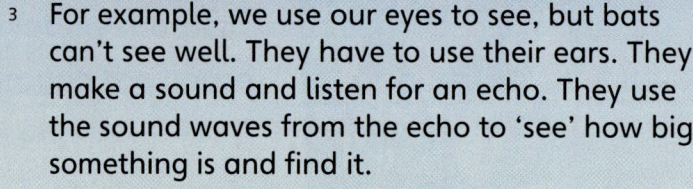

1. Do you know what senses are for? Every minute of every day our senses get information and send it to our brain. We use this information to understand the world around us. With our senses we understand when food looks, smells, or tastes good and fresh, or when it's bad and rotten. We also feel something hot or sharp or hear when danger is coming with our senses. Our senses are very important because they keep us safe.

2. Like people, animals use their senses to find food and avoid danger. But many animals' senses are very different from people's senses.

3. For example, we use our eyes to see, but bats can't see well. They have to use their ears. They make a sound and listen for an echo. They use the sound waves from the echo to 'see' how big something is and find it.

4. Snakes and lizards don't smell with their noses like us; they smell with their tongues! That's why their tongues are like a fork. The fork shape helps them understand where a smell is coming from.

5. Butterflies, on the other hand, don't taste with their tongues; they use their feet. They have tiny taste buds there. They help the butterfly understand what flower it is standing on. That's how they know they can eat it.

6. Maybe we see with our noses or feel with our ears. It doesn't matter. The message to our brain is the important thing. Our brain helps us understand all the messages our senses send us.

THINK BIG Why do animals use their senses differently from people? Which sense is the most important? Why?

15 Look at 14. Read and match.

1 We use our senses
2 Animals use their senses
3 Bats use sound
4 Snakes use their tongues
5 Butterflies use their feet
6 Our brains help us

a to taste things.
b understand messages from our senses.
c to smell things.
d to find food.
e to understand the size of something.
f to understand if something is dangerous for us.

16 Complete the chart. Which senses do you use for each of these things?

Go to a concert	Eat dinner in a restaurant	Play with a pet	Go on a roller coaster ride
?	?	?	?

PROJECT

17 Find out about other animal senses and make an **Animal Senses** poster. Then present it to the class.

A chameleon can move its eyes in different directions. It uses its tongue to catch its food and taste it.

Grammar

18 **Look, listen, and read. Is the milkshake sweet?**

Scott: I drink a milkshake at school every day. But this is my delicious new chocolate milkshake recipe. First of all, how does it smell?

Emily: Hmm. It smells chocolatey.

Scott: Yes, it has chocolate in. Now try it. How does it taste?

Emily: It tastes cold. But yuck! It doesn't taste sweet. It tastes salty! What's in it?

Scott: Oh, no! I put salt in instead of sugar!

This	is	a milkshake.		
I	drink	it	at school	every day.
It	smells	chocolatey.		
It	doesn't taste	sweet.		

19 Complete the chart using the words from the box.

> bitter   hard   hot   rough   salty   soft   sweet

Feel	Taste	Both
smooth	spicy	cold
sharp	sour	?
?	?	
?	?	
?	?	

98 Unit 6

Grammar

20 Put the words in order. Then say.

1. cakes | My mom's | delicious. | taste
2. in a bakery | Dad | on Tuesdays. | works
3. from the supermarket | We | flowers | every day. | buy
4. eating bones. | doesn't like | My dog
5. taste buds | on their feet. | Butterflies | have
6. eats | two mice | every week. | The snake

21 Read and choose the correct answer.

1. When do you get up in the morning?
   a I every day get up at 6 o' clock.
   b I get up at 6 o' clock every day.
   c At 6 o' clock I get up every day.
2. Where do you eat breakfast?
   a I eat at the zoo café eggs on toast.
   b I eat eggs on toast at the zoo café.
   c At the zoo café I eat eggs on toast.
3. What's your first job?
   a The snakes cages I clean.
   b I the snakes cages clean.
   c I clean the snakes cages.
4. How do they feel?
   a They're feeling smooth.
   b They are feel smooth.
   c They feel smooth.
5. Are the snakes dangerous?
   a No. The snakes friendly!
   b Snakes they are friendly.
   c No. The snakes are friendly.
6. How do they smell?
   a They smell not bad.
   b They don't smell bad.
   c They are smell bad.

22 Play a game. Choose an object. Don't tell your partner. Ask and answer.

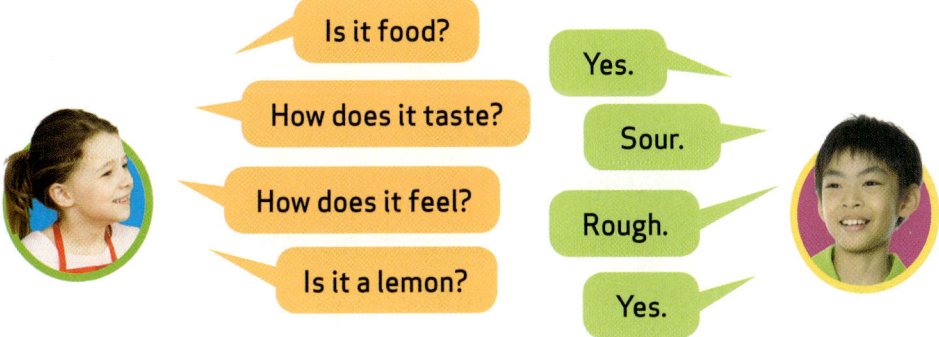

Culture Connection | Around the World

How Does Your Job Smell?

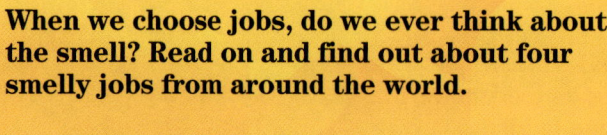

When we choose jobs, do we ever think about the smell? Read on and find out about four smelly jobs from around the world.

1 André Tyrode is from Lyon. He makes cakes and pastries every day. "Everything I make tastes and smells wonderful. It makes people want to share delicious treats together, and that makes them happy. And if they're happy, I'm happy!"

Is there anything bad about his job? Well, he gets up at 5:00 a.m. every day, and he usually feels very tired, but the smell of fresh bread always makes him smile.

2 Alberto Rivera from Costa Rica likes his job because he can look at flowers all day. He grows and sells flowers on his farm, then sends them all over the world. "When you see all the different colors, it really helps you remember how beautiful the world is."

Do all the flowers smell good? Yes, they do, but smelling that many flowers sometimes makes Alberto sneeze!

23 You have one minute. Think of three smells that make you really happy and three smells you hate. Write them in your notebook and compare them with a partner.

24 Listen and read. Say whether each person's job has a good smell or a bad smell. Then match the jobs **a–d** below to the people **1–4**.

a Baker
b Zoo keeper
c Garbage collector
d Farmer

CONTENT WORDS
clean   awful   fresh   smelly
stink   take care of   wet

25 Look at **24**. Which person: André, Alberto, Candace, or Sarah...

1 creates something beautiful?
2 improves a place?
3 gets up early regularly?
4 sometimes gets very wet at work?
5 works with other countries?
6 has a problem with his nose because of his job?
7 makes something people can share?
8 lives in a very clean city?

3 Candace Reilly is from Calgary, a city in Canada. She does a very important job. She picks trash and helps keep her city clean. Today, Calgary is the cleanest city in Canada! What does she say about a job like that? "My job doesn't smell great, in fact the trash really stinks, but I like making Calgary look, feel, and smell cleaner and better."

4 Sarah Ang takes care of Zelda, the Asian elephant at Singapore Zoo. It's one of the largest in the world. "Sometimes Zelda smells, and I have to give her a bath. It's actually a great feeling when you take care of an animal like Zelda, but the smell is really awful." The bad thing is that when Sarah gives Zelda a bath, she has to take a bath, too. Luckily Singapore is hot and wet.

Which job would you do?

26 **Look at 24. Which job would you like/hate to do? Why? Compare your answers with a partner.**

I would like to be a flower farmer. Flowers smell good!

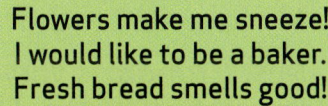

Flowers make me sneeze! I would like to be a baker. Fresh bread smells good!

27 **Look at 26. In your notebook, write about a typical day in your job. Compare with a partner.**

THINK BIG Why do some people do jobs that aren't very nice? Imagine these people do the same jobs in other countries around the world. Are the smells the same?

Writing | Paragraph: Final Sentences

28 Read and complete with **topic sentence**, **detail sentences**, and **final sentence**.

> A paragraph begins with a ¹ ❓ . It introduces the subject of the paragraph.
>
> > I love tomatoes.
>
> ² ❓ expand on your topic by giving details about it.
>
> > Home-grown tomatoes taste delicious, and they're good for you.
> > Fresh tomatoes right from the garden smell great.
> > They look nice in a salad, too.
>
> You end your paragraph with a ³ ❓ . It expresses the same idea as your topic sentence but in a different way.
>
> > Of all fruits and vegetables, tomatoes are my favorite.

29 Read the paragraphs. Find the best **final sentence** for each one.

1. **Topic Sentence:** My favorite toy is my teddy bear, Simpson.
   Detail Sentences: Simpson is very old. He doesn't look very nice. But I like him very much. He feels soft, and he always smells so nice. He can't talk or run, but that's OK.

   Final Sentence:
   a Simpson is just an old teddy bear.
   b I love Simpson more than any of my other toys.
   c Simpson doesn't do a lot.

2. **Topic Sentence:** My favorite teacher is Mrs. Graham.
   Detail Sentences: Mrs. Graham is very nice. She teaches us many interesting things. She never gets angry. Mrs. Graham is friendly, and she smiles a lot.

   Final Sentence:
   a Mrs. Graham is 40 years old.
   b Mrs. Graham doesn't like cake very much.
   c Mrs. Graham is the best teacher at our school.

30 Write a **final sentence** for this paragraph.

> Fall is my favorite season. The colorful leaves on the trees look so pretty. The air feels nice and cool, and the fall smells great.

fl, pl, gl, bl | Phonics

 31 **Listen, read, and repeat.**

1 **fl** 2 **pl** 3 **gl** 4 **bl**

 **32** **Listen and find. Then say.**

flip-**fl**ops   **pl**um   **gl**ass   **bl**ack

 33 **Listen and blend the sounds.**

1 f-l-a-g   flag   2 p-l-a-n-t   plant
3 p-l-ay   play   4 f-l-y   fly
5 g-l-a-d   glad   6 g-l-ow   glow
7 b-l-o-ck block   8 b-l-ow   blow

 34 **Read aloud. Then listen and chant.**

It's summer.
Yellow plums,
Green plants.
Flip-flops,
Black shorts,
It's summer.
I'm glad!

Values | Try new things.

35 Look, listen, and point.

a
b
c

36 Practice with a partner. Talk about something new that you want to try.

My mom showed me how to make oatmeal cookies. Do you want to make them with me?

OK!

PROJECT

37 Work with a group. Make a **Try New Things** flip chart.

Try New Things

bake cookies

104 Unit 6 values

Review

38 Look at the pictures. Complete the questions. Then say.

1 How does the ice cream 🔔 ?
2 How does the rock band 🔔 ?
3 How does the man 🔔 ?
4 How does the stuffed animal 🔔 ?
5 How do the flowers 🔔 ?

39 Make answers for **38**.

40 Correct the sentences.

1 Butterflies taste with their tongues.
2 Snakes and lizards smell with their legs.
3 To taste, bats use their ears.
4 Chameleons have very short tongues.

41 Put the words in order. Then say.

1 | an apple | every day. | on the playground | I eat |
2 | in the bathroom | Leyla brushes | after breakfast. | her teeth |
3 | at 9 p.m. | I watch | in my room | my favorite TV show |
4 | My mom | to work | at 7:30 a.m. | drives |

I Can

- describe how things look, feel, taste, smell, or sound.
- talk about the five senses in people and animals.
- find and use final sentences.

Checkpoint | Units 4–6

How Well Do I Know It? Can I Use It?

1 Think about it. Read and draw. Practice.

😊 I know this.   😐 I need more practice.   😟 I don't know this.

		PAGES			
1	**Animals:** deer, owl, camel, lizard…	58	😊	😐	😟
2	**Habitats:** lake, ocean, rain forest…	59	😊	😐	😟
3	**Weather:** hot, cold, windy, rainy…	74	😊	😐	😟
4	**Clothes:** coat, sweater, scarf…	75	😊	😐	😟
5	**Describing:** awful, delicious, nice, pretty…	90	😊	😐	😟
6	What **can** penguins do? They **can** swim, but they **can't** fly.	62–63	😊	😐	😟
7	David is loud. He speaks **loudly**.	66–67	😊	😐	😟
8	What is the weather like **today**? **It's** hot and sunny.	78–79	😊	😐	😟
9	It **was** cold yesterday. We **were** freezing.	82–83	😊	😐	😟
10	How **does** the apple pie **taste**? It **tastes** delicious.	94–95	😊	😐	😟
11	I drink milk at school every day. The shoes feel tight at night.	98–99	😊	😐	😟

I Can Do It!

2 **Get ready.**

A Complete the dialog. Use the words from the box. Then listen and check.

> awful   cold   fly
> look   swim

Morgan: Look at those penguins!
Taylor: They ¹ ❓ cool!
Morgan: Yeah. I like penguins. Hey, look at this: "Penguins live in the snow and ice."
Taylor: That sounds ² ❓ !
Morgan: Yes, very cold. Listen. "They eat fish every day." Look. They're eating fish now!
Taylor: Yuck! That looks ³ ❓ to me!
Morgan: Well, the penguins like it.
Taylor: Hey, look. They're swimming.
Morgan: Yes, penguins can ⁴ ❓ . But they can't ⁵ ❓ .
Taylor: Wow. I'm learning a lot about penguins!

B Practice the dialog in **A** with a partner. Then practice again. Talk about different animals.

C Choose the words for you.
1 I **like/don't like** penguins.
2 Their food looks **delicious/terrible** to me.
3 Their home looks **warm/cold** to me.

Checkpoint Units 4–6 **107**

Checkpoint | Units 4–6

3 Get set.

 STEP 1 Look and read. Find out information about an animal.

 STEP 2 Cut out the book outline on page 159 of your Workbook. Fold it to make a book.

 STEP 3 Write in your own animal information book. Now you're ready to **Go!**

4 Go!

A Swap books with five classmates. Write notes about their books in your notebook.

Classmate	Animal	Comment
Carla	lizards	great

B Tell the class about some of your classmates' books.

Elena's book was about sharks. Sharks are amazing!

5 **Write about yourself in your notebook.**

- What was the weather like today?
- What was the weather like yesterday?
- Today I can…
- Today I can't…

- Today the sky looks…
- My classroom feels…
- My favorite animal is…
- I like this animal because…

All About Me   Date:

How Well Do I Know It Now?

6 **Think about it. Look at page 106 and your notebook. Draw again.**

  A Use a different color.

  B Read and think.
   I can start the next unit.
   I can ask my teacher for help and then start the next unit.
   I can practice and then start the next unit.

7 **Rate this Checkpoint.**

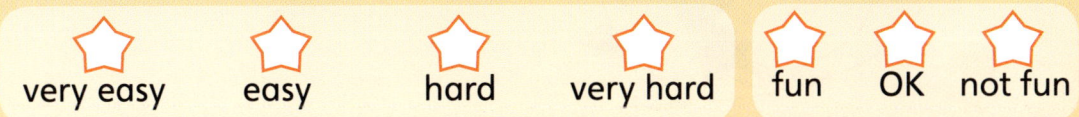

very easy   easy   hard   very hard   fun   OK   not fun

Checkpoint Units 4–6 **109**

Units 4–6 Exam Preparation

– Part A –

Listen, color, and draw. There is one example.

110 Listening part 5

– Part B –

Read the text and choose the best answer. Jack is talking to his friend, Daisy.

Example

Jack: What's the weather like?
Daisy: A I like it when it's sunny.
 Ⓑ It's cloudy but warm.
 C It was hot yesterday.

Questions

1 **Jack:** Would you like to go to the lake?
 Daisy: A Yes, there's a lake.
 B Yes, you do.
 C Yes, I'd like that.

3 **Jack:** What does the ice cream taste like?
 Daisy: A Are you hungry?
 B It tastes nice!
 C The ice cream is cold.

5 **Jack:** Do we need a sweater?
 Daisy: A He needs a coat.
 B I like your sweater.
 C I think so, yes.

2 **Jack:** What can we do there?
 Daisy: A We can feed the fish.
 B We can do that.
 C We can go there.

4 **Jack:** Should we ride our bikes there?
 Daisy: A Great idea!
 B Mine is blue.
 C Yes, I can.

6 **Jack:** Is your brother coming?
 Daisy: A No, he has to study.
 B No, he wasn't here yesterday.
 C No, he works in a store.

Unit 7 Fabulous Food!

 1 **Listen, look, and say.**

At *Your Way Café* you decide what to put in your sandwich or on your pizza. There are so many things to choose from. Which will you choose?

1 Super Sandwiches!

1 bread   2 cucumbers   3 turkey   4 mustard   5 lettuce

2 Pizza Perfection!

6 green peppers   7 mushrooms   8 tomato sauce   9 olives   10 onions

 **2** **Listen, find, and say.**   **3** **Play a game.**

112 Unit 7 vocabulary (food)

 **4** Listen and sing. What do they eat?

I'm Hungry!

Hi, Mom, I'm home from school.
I'm really hungry now.
I'd like to make a sandwich,
Can you show me how?

I am home from my school day.
I'd like a sandwich. Is that OK?

Are there any olives?
Here are some on the shelf.
Is there any tomato sauce?
I see it for myself.

Chorus

There's just one problem, Mom
There isn't any bread!
But I have a great idea:
Let's have pizza instead!

Chorus

 5 Look at **1**. Ask and answer.

 What do you like in your sandwiches?

I like turkey and lettuce.

 What is good on pizzas and in sandwiches?

Story

6 Listen and read. What are Luke and Amy making?

A Surprise for Mom

1 Luke and Amy are making dinner for their mom. It's a surprise.

2 They need toppings for their pizza.

3 Amy and Luke taste some of the pizza toppings.

4 They look in the fridge again. What can they use?

5 Amy and Luke look for more food.

6 There's a surprise for Mom in the kitchen, but it isn't dinner.

7 Read and say true or false.

1 Amy and Luke want to make breakfast for their mother.
2 There aren't any onions for the pizza.
3 Amy and Luke eat all the cheese and olives.
4 There isn't any turkey.
5 There isn't a surprise for Mom.

THINK BIG What do you think Amy and Luke's mom does next? Why? How can they help their mom?

Language in Action

8 Listen and look at the sentences. Help Luke and Amy make more.

turkey   tomatoes   bread   mushrooms

There's some cheese.
There isn't any cheese.
Is there any cheese?
There are some olives.
There aren't any olives.
Are there any olives?

9 Read and choose.

1 There's **some/any** tomato sauce on the pizza.
2 There are **some/any** sandwiches in my bag.
3 There aren't **some/any** olives in the kitchen.
4 There isn't **some/any** lettuce in my sandwich.
5 Are there **any/some** olives? Yes, there are.
6 **Is/Are** there any cheese? Yes, there is.

10 Make the questions.

1 No, there isn't. There isn't any bread.
2 Yes, there are some bananas. I think there are four.
3 Yes, there is. The lettuce is in the fridge.
4 No, there aren't any mushrooms in the soup. Don't worry!
5 Yes, there are some strawberries. They're next to the mangoes.

Language in Action

11 Complete the dialog in pairs. Then listen and check.

Rob: Mom, can we have pizza for dinner?

Mom: Good idea. Look in the fridge. Is there ¹ ❓ tomato sauce?

Rob: Yes, there ² ❓ .

Mom: Is ³ ❓ any cheese?

Rob: Yes, there is. There are ⁴ ❓ mushrooms and some onions.

Mom: Great! What about olives? ⁵ ❓ there ⁶ ❓ olives?

Rob: No, there ⁷ ❓ .

Mom: That's OK, Dad doesn't like olives. We can have pizza for dinner.

Rob: Great! Let's start now.

12 Look and make sentences in pairs. There is the food in blue and there isn't the food in red.

bananas   bread   cheese   cucumbers   lettuce   mushrooms

 There's…   … some cheese.

13 Look. Ask and answer about the sandwich.

Is there any turkey for your sandwich?

Yes, there is.

Are there any mushrooms for your sandwich?

No, there aren't.

Content Connection | Science

14 Work with a partner. Guess if these statements are true or false.

1. You can only find vitamins in fruit and vegetables.
2. There aren't any vitamins in chocolate.
3. There's a lot of vitamin A in orange fruits and vegetables.
4. The human body can make vitamin D.
5. All vitamins live inside our bodies for years.

15 Listen and read. How many different fruit and vegetables should we eat each day? Then check your answers in 14.

CONTENT WORDS
blood   bone   brain   energy   fat/water soluble
healthy   iron   muscle   skin   teeth   vitamin

The Vitamin Alphabet

Vitamins help our bodies grow strong and stay healthy. We need vitamins every day, and we have to get them from the food we eat. There are two types of vitamins. Some of them live in the fat in our body and stay in our bodies. Others live in the water in our bodies. They don't stay around for long. But which foods do we get our vitamins from? And why do we need them?

Let's start with the fat soluble vitamins: A, D, and E.

Vitamin A: There's a lot of Vitamin A in orange and yellow fruits like carrots or mangoes, but you can also find some in milk and the yellow part of eggs. Vitamin A helps your eyes and skin stay healthy.

Vitamin D: Milk and eggs also have Vitamin D in them, and so does fish. When we sit in the sun, our body makes a lot of it naturally. This vitamin is very important for strong bones.

Vitamin E: This, on the other hand, helps keep our blood healthy. You can get Vitamin E when you eat nuts and green vegetables.

The water soluble Vitamins B and C are just as important.

Vitamin B: There are many different kinds of Vitamin B. Some help give us energy to move our muscles. Others help make blood. We get the different kinds of Vitamin B from different kinds of food. These include potatoes, bananas, bread, rice, pasta, chicken, fish, cheese, eggs, and green peppers.

Vitamin C: Vitamin C is good for our bones, teeth, and even our brains. We get this vitamin from oranges, peppers, tomatoes, and potatoes. Vitamin C also helps us keep other important substances, iron for example, in our body.

We should eat a good variety of fruit and vegetables – at least five a day – and lots of other healthy foods like brown bread, milk, eggs, and fish. That way, we always get the vitamins we need. But we can eat some 'bad' things too. For example, there are three B vitamins in a good bar of dark chocolate!

 **Which vitamins do the following people need and why?**
a a soccer player   b a pilot

16 **Look at 15. Read and answer the questions. Write the answers in your notebook.**

1. What are the two types of vitamins?
2. How are they different?
3. Is it more important to eat one group every day? Why?
4. Why is it good to get lots of Vitamin A?
5. Which foods contain Vitamin E?
6. Which vitamin has lots of different ones?
7. Which vitamin do we get from the sun?

17 **Where do you get your vitamins from? Complete the chart. Tell your partner.**

	Food	Vitamins
Breakfast		
Snack		
Lunch		
Dinner		

PROJECT

18 **Imagine you're teaching other children about vitamins and where you find them. Make a Vitamin Plate, and present it to the class. Make sure you include all the vitamins and different food groups.**

There are carrots on my plate because there's a lot of Vitamin A in carrots. Vitamin A is good for our skin.

Grammar

19 **Look, listen, and read. Does Dan have a healthy dinner?**

Jenna: Is that your dinner? There's a lot of meat and a lot of bread, but there isn't much fruit, and there aren't many vegetables!

Dan: There are some vegetables with my meal. Look, there's an onion, and I have a few potatoes. There's also a little lettuce and ketchup on my burger. How many vegetables do I have to eat?

Jenna: Well, there aren't many vitamins in those! Look! You have to eat a lot of fruit and vegetables to get your vitamins!

Dan: That's OK. You have a big salad and some fruit. You can eat the vitamins for me!

You have **a** big salad. I have **an** onion. You have **some** fruit. There's **a lot of** meat. There's **a little** ketchup.	There are **some** vegetables with my meal. You have to eat **a lot of** vegetables. I have **a few** potatoes.
There isn't **much** fruit.	There aren't **many** vegetables.
How much fruit do I have to eat?	**How many** vegetables do I have to eat?

20 **Read and choose.**

1 There's **an/a** orange in my bag.
2 There isn't **some/much** cheese on this pizza!
3 I don't like **many/much** pizza toppings.
4 Can I have **a/some** glass of milk?
5 Mom makes **a lot of/a few** food for birthday parties.
6 There are only **a few/a little** vitamins in chocolate.
7 I don't eat **some/much** bread for breakfast.
8 Please put **a few/some** sugar on my cereal.

Grammar

21 Complete the statements with **much**, **many**, **a little**, or **a few**.

1. I don't eat ? chips. They aren't good for you.
2. I eat ? chocolate every day – it's healthy.
3. There aren't ? vitamins in popcorn.
4. Dad drinks ? cups of coffee a day. Is that bad?
5. I don't eat ? cheese. There's a lot of fat in it.
6. Mom says I can't have ? ketchup on my burger. Why not?

22 Complete the quiz questions. Use **How much** or **How many**.

1. ? meat do you eat?
2. ? times a week do you eat fish?
3. ? fruit and vegetables do you eat every day?
4. ? healthy snacks do you eat?
5. ? fizzy drinks or desserts do you have each day?
6. ? exercise do you do?

23 Complete Keira's answer to the quiz questions.

> a few (x2)   little   lot of (x2)   many   much (x2)   some

I don't eat ¹ ? meat because I don't really like it. I eat fish though. I think fish is delicious. Every day, I eat ² ? fruit, and I eat a ³ ? vegetables, too, because I don't like meat. I eat one small snack in the morning, usually ⁴ ? nuts or sometimes a ⁵ ? yogurt. I know I sound like a goody goody, but I really don't eat ⁶ ? chocolate. Not ⁷ ? teenagers can say that! And I only drink ⁸ ? fizzy drinks because I only drink them at parties. And of course, I do a ⁹ ? exercise. I'm on the swim team!

24 Now ask and answer the quiz questions in **22** with a partner. Then write about your answers in your notebook.

> I eat a little meat. I like eating some chicken or a burger once or twice a week.

grammar (*You have some fruit. There aren't many potatoes.*) Unit 7

Culture Connection | Around the World

Breakfast in Different Countries. What do you get?

Katie, UK

Today I'm writing about breakfast. My mom says breakfast is the most important meal of the day, so she puts a healthy breakfast on the table every day at 7:30 a.m. On school days, we eat cereal with milk and a banana, hard-boiled eggs, and brown bread soldiers, or just toast with marmite. On Saturdays or Sundays, we usually have bacon and tomato butties with a few strawberries or blueberries on the side. That tastes great! But this Saturday morning, breakfast was awful! It was porridge – yuck. That's oat cereal with hot milk. Mom loves it, and she eats it every day with some honey. But why do we have to eat it? And on a Saturday, too! What do you all eat for breakfast?

Yoko, Japan

That sounds OK! My family never eats any cereal. In the morning, I usually eat rice, soup, fish, and pickles.

25 Discuss with a partner.
1 Do you eat breakfast every day?
2 What time do you usually eat it?
3 What are some of the things that people eat for breakfast in your country?
4 What's your favorite breakfast on weekends?

26 Listen and read Katie's blog. What does she say about her breakfast today?

> **CONTENT WORDS**
> blueberries   cereal   donut   hard-boiled/fried eggs
> honey   oats   porridge   toast

27 Look at 26. Answer the questions in 25 for Katie.

28 Look and match the breakfasts to the correct country.

1 UK   2 Japan   3 Mexico   4 Australia   5 Spain

a
b
c
d
e

122 Unit 7

Luis, Spain

I like fish, but I never eat it for breakfast! I usually eat bread or cereal for breakfast, too, but sometimes on weekends, I eat churros with chocolate. Churros are like little donuts. They're delicious!

Camilla, Mexico

We often eat eggs for breakfast, but they aren't hard-boiled. They're fried. They're called huevos rancheros. We put them on toasted tortillas with some salsa. They are spicy, colorful, and delicious! What's marmite?

Tony, Australia

Marmite is brown and salty, and you can put it on your toast. We eat it here, too, but it's called Vegemite :-). We sometimes eat porridge, too, I think it's OK. I put cream and a little brown sugar on top. But I really like eating toast in the morning – with beans on top! Yum! Do you eat that in the UK?

Katie, UK

Thanks for writing everybody. Huevos rancheros and churros with chocolate sound yummy!

29 Think about these questions. Then compare with a partner.
1 Which breakfast do you like? Why?
2 Which breakfast don't you like? Why?
3 Which breakfast is healthy?
4 Which breakfast isn't healthy?

30 Find out about breakfasts in three other countries. Share with the class.

In Turkey, people eat cheese, olives, and salad for breakfast.

THINK BIG Why is it important to eat a good breakfast? Where do people eat these for breakfast? Find out!
   a kippers   **b** kimchi   **c** potato pancakes

Writing | Paragraphs

31 Listen and read. Then match.

> **Title** – says what you are writing about
> **Topic sentence** – explains the main idea
> **Detail sentences** – add more information
> **Final sentence** – summarizes and gives an opinion

detail sentences   final sentence   title   topic sentence

1 **My Favorite Breakfast**
by Laura Brown

2 I like a lot of different things for breakfast, but I have my favorite breakfast every Sunday morning.

3 I start with some orange slices, cold from the fridge. Then my mother makes two fluffy pancakes for me. I put butter on them, and then I put warm maple syrup on top. The pancakes are delicious with a glass of cold milk.

4 My favorite breakfast makes Sundays special.

Writing Steps

32 **Write about your favorite breakfast.**
1. Think about your favorite breakfast.
2. Write a title.
3. Write a topic sentence.
4. Add details to give more information.
5. Write a final sentence.

br, cr, dr, fr, gr, pr, tr | Phonics

33 **Listen, read, and repeat.**

1 br 2 cr 3 dr 4 fr 5 gr 6 pr 7 tr

34 **Listen and find. Then say.**

bread **cr**eam **dr**eam **fr**og

grass **pr**ize **tr**ain

35 **Listen and blend the sounds.**

1 d-r-i-ve   drive   2 g-r-ee-n   green
3 b-r-ow-n   brown   4 p-r-i-n-ce   prince
5 c-r-y   cry   6 t-r-o-ll   troll
7 f-r-o-m   from   8 b-r-i-ck   brick

36 **Read aloud. Then listen and chant.**

Every night,
I dream
About a prince
And a troll,
And a green frog!
In my dream,
They eat bread
With cream.

Values | Try different foods.

 **37** Listen. Look at the poster. Which dish looks good to you? Discuss with a partner.

Peruvians love potatoes. Peru grows more than 2,300 types of potatoes. There are many different shapes, sizes, and colors!

Potatoes grow very well in the cool weather, high in the Andes Mountains.

Potatoes in Peru

The most famous dish is *papa a la huancaína* – potatoes in a spicy cheese sauce.

Another is *papa rellena*, or stuffed potato. This dish has meat, onions, and eggs stuffed inside a potato.

 I want to try the stuffed potato. It looks delicious!

 **PROJECT**

38 Make a poster about the food in a country other than your own.

1. Learn about the typical foods in that country.
2. Cut out pictures of the foods.
3. Label the pictures.
4. Share your poster with the class.

CHINA — noodles, dumplings, fried rice

Review

39 Read and match.

1 I have a
2 They eat a lot of
3 I don't like many salads.
4 How much salt is in this?
5 How many slices do you want?

a Only a few seem tasty to me.
b big pizza.
c I've put only a little.
d Three, please.
e oranges.

40 Read and choose. Then role-play.

Juanita: Hi, Mom. I'm really hungry. Can I have a snack, please?
Mom: Have some fruit.
Juanita: **Is/Are** there any strawberries?
Mom: I don't think so.
Juanita: Is there **any/some** pineapple?
Mom: No, there isn't. What about an apple?
Juanita: Is there any **cheese/olives**?
Mom: Yes, there **is/isn't**.
Juanita: Great. A cheese sandwich!
Mom: Sorry, but there **isn't/aren't** any bread.
Juanita: Well, I think I'll have an apple then.

41 Make a pizza. Ask and answer to find two people with the same pizza. Use the words from the box.

> cheese   chicken   cucumbers   mushrooms   olives
> onion   peppers   tomato sauce   turkey

Is there any cheese on your pizza?

Yes, there is.

I Can

- ask and answer about food.
- talk about vitamins and how they help my body.
- find different parts of a paragraph.

Unit 8 Healthy Living

1 Listen, look, and say.

How do you feel today? Find out how healthy Sally and Zach are, then ask yourself!

I feel great today.

1 Did she... have a big breakfast?

2 Did she... get 10 hours of sleep last night?

3 Did she... drink lots of water?

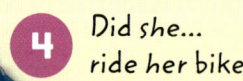
4 Did she... ride her bike?

5 Did he... eat breakfast?

6 Did he... get any exercise?

7 Did he... have a healthy lunch?

8 Did he... get enough sleep?

2 Listen, find, and say.   **3** Play a game.

4 Listen and sing. How does Zach feel today?

Live Right!

Did you eat breakfast? asks Mom,
You don't look good to me.
Did you get enough sleep? asks Mom,
Did you watch too much TV?

**Enough sleep. Good food.
Be healthy. Live right!
Enough sleep. Good food.
Be healthy. Live right!**

Did you ride your bike? asks Mom,
You know it's good for you.
Did you get any exercise?
You know it's good to do!

Chorus

I feel awful today.

5 Look at 1. Ask and answer.

Did he eat breakfast?

Did she ride her bike?

No, he didn't.

Yes, she did.

THINK BIG Which child in 1 are you like? Explain why.

Story

 Listen and read. Did Amy eat a healthy dinner?

1 Amy's dad wants her to be healthy.

2 Amy likes unhealthy food.

3 Amy likes fries, but fried food isn't very healthy.

4 Amy likes cola.

5 Amy knows her dinner wasn't really healthy. She didn't eat many vegetables.

6 Now Amy doesn't feel well. She needs to eat healthy food.

7 Read and choose.

1 Amy had dinner at a **party/home**.
2 Amy likes **healthy/unhealthy** food.
3 Fries are fried **potatoes/onions**.
4 Fried food is **good/bad** for you.
5 Cola has a lot of **fruit/sugar** in it.
6 Amy's dad **is/isn't** happy about Amy's dinner.

THINK BIG What should Amy eat for her next dinner? Why?

Language in Action

8 Listen and look at the sentences. Help Luke and Amy make more.

drink lots of water   eat a healthy lunch

get enough exercise

Did you have breakfast ?
No , I didn't .
Did he get enough sleep ?
Yes , he did .

9 Match the phrases. Make five questions about yesterday. Then ask and answer.

1 do any
2 drink lots
3 have a
4 get enough
5 ride

a of water
b healthy lunch
c sleep
d my bike
e exercise

Did you do any exercise yesterday?

No, I didn't.

Language in Action

10 **Complete the dialogs. Use did or didn't.**

1. **A:** Good morning, Katia. ❓ you eat breakfast?
   B: Yes, I ❓.
2. **A:** ❓ Ted take a shower this morning?
   B: No, he ❓.
3. **A:** ❓ the soccer team get enough sleep before the game?
   B: No, they ❓.
4. **A:** ❓ Melissa brush her teeth?
   B: Yes, she ❓.

11 **Put the words in order to make questions. Then ask.**

1. yesterday? | Did | get | enough | Alice | sleep
2. play soccer | last week? | Did | after school | they
3. a shower | Did | take | this morning? | you
4. play | video games | weekend? | we | Did | on the
5. on Sunday? | go | Matthew | Did | to the park

12 **Read and match. Now change the answers.**

1. Did Ruth visit her cousin yesterday?
2. Did you go to a national park?
3. Did Mike like the band?
4. Did your mom and dad watch a DVD?
5. Did Melanie have onions on her pizza?
6. Did you learn a lot at school today?

a. Yes, they did. It was great.
b. Yes, I did. I learned about healthy and unhealthy food.
c. No, she didn't. She hates them!
d. Yes, she did. She was glad to see her.
e. No, he didn't. He doesn't like going to concerts.
f. No, we didn't. It was too cold and snowy.

language practice (Yes, I did./No, I didn't.) Unit 8

Content Connection | P.E.

13 Read, guess, and choose.

1. How much exercise is good for children?
   a 60 minutes or more every day
   b 30 minutes three times a week

2. Which activity uses more energy?
   a playing computer games
   b playing soccer

14 Listen and read. What are the numbers 60, 12,000, 9, and 10? Then check your answers in 13.

What Is a Calorie?

CONTENT WORDS
active   activities   body   burn   calorie
in shape   measure   put on weight   rest

www.teen_health.org

Exercise, eating, and sleeping are important parts of our daily routine. Exercise every day for at least 60 minutes. Eat the correct number of calories so that you have the energy to exercise. Get the correct amount of rest. Read on to answer some simple questions.

What are calories? Are they important?
A calorie is a measure of the energy you get from food. Some foods are high in calories, and other foods aren't. Your body needs a certain number of calories to do all the things you do every day. But if you eat more calories than your body needs, you put on too much weight. Lots of activity and exercise burns a lot of calories. Very little activity or exercise doesn't burn a lot of calories. For example, Michael Phelps, the Olympic Swimmer, ate 12,000 calories every day during the Olympic Games, but he didn't put on weight because he burned all the calories!

Why is being active good for us?
It helps our hearts stay healthy. It makes our bones strong, and it creates muscles. Being active is really important for young and old people. Activities that use lots of energy are best. Dancing is really good for your body. Riding a bike and swimming are also good for your body. But watching TV or playing video games are bad for your health if you do them too much. That's because you sit in the same place to do them.

Is there a right amount of sleep?
Yes. Sleeping is good for your health, but sleeping too much or too little is definitely bad for you. Doctors say between 9 and 10 hours of sleep is best for teenagers. When we sleep, we rest our bodies and our brains. Then we're ready for activity again the next day.

Paying attention to what exercise you do helps you stay in shape. How much do you do? How much time do you spend in front of the TV or computer? How many hours a night do you sleep? Do you eat the right things? Be honest!

THINK BIG How do you feel when you sleep too little or too much? Why is it bad for you?

15 Look at **14**. Answer the questions in your notebook.

1. What's a calorie?
2. Why do people put on weight?
3. Why didn't Michael Phelps put on weight?
4. What does exercise or activity do for our bodies?
5. Why is watching TV or playing video games unhealthy?

16 Complete the chart. Use the activities from the box. Then add more activities.

> dancing   playing a sport   playing video games   riding my bike to school
> sleeping for 13 hours   watching TV

Good for your body	Bad for your body

17 Work with a partner. Ask and answer the questions at the end of the article in **14**.

> How much exercise do you do?

PROJECT

18 Make an **Exercise Chart** for you. Show good activities and bad activities. Are you healthy and in shape?

Day of the week	Activity	Number of hours	Good or bad
On Monday	Dancing	2 hours	Good – dancing is good for you. It keeps you in shape and burns calories.

> I ride my bike to school every day, and I swim twice a week. I play soccer every Saturday, too.

content connection (keeping healthy) Unit 8

Grammar

19 Look, listen, and read. How did Donna's dad come home?

Donna: In 2005, my dad was a champion cyclist, but he stopped in 2007 because he hurt his knee. Last week, the doctor said his knee was better. Yesterday, Dad started a new healthy living program. He went to bed early, and he slept for eight hours. When he got up, he ate a good healthy breakfast, he made a healthy lunch, he put it in his backpack, and he rode his bicycle to work. He rode ten kilometers to work, and then he rode another ten kilometers home.

Brad: Wow! I saw a man with a fantastic bicycle an hour ago. He looked in really good shape. Was that your dad?

Donna: No. Dad came home two hours ago. When he arrived, he sat on the couch, and he fell asleep right away!

	I/You/He/She/It/We/They	play**ed**. walk**ed**. stay**ed**.
	start – **ed** cr**y** – **ied** lik**e** – **d** st**op** – **ped**	start**ed** cr**ied** lik**ed** stop**ped**
But...	I/You/He/She/It/We/They	**went**. **saw**. **came**.

20 Copy the chart in your notebook and complete. Use the words from the box.

> bake   carry   change   climb   cry   drop   exercise
> finish   help   join   love   tip   try   worry

start**ed**	cr**ied**	lik**ed**	stop**ped**
?	?	?	?

Grammar

21 Read and complete.

1
Ffyona Campbell's dad ¹ (work) for the Royal Navy. When she was a little girl, she ² (move) to a new house 24 times and ³ (live) in a lot of different countries. When Ffyona was 21, she ⁴ (travel) across Australia on foot. She ⁵ (walk) 50 miles a day for 95 days and ⁶ (complete) 32,000 miles from Sydney to Perth.

2
In November 2012, Okan Kaya from Australia ⁷ (play) the longest video game marathon. It ⁸ (last) 135 hours, 15 minutes, and 10 seconds. He only ⁹ (stop) the game after seven days.

22 Read and match.

1 go
2 come
3 have
4 sleep
5 fall
6 write
7 fly
8 put

a wrote
b slept
c put
d went
e had
f came
g flew
h fell

23 Tell your partner about what you did yesterday.

Yesterday, I woke up early and walked to school.

Yesterday, I went to the park after school. I played soccer.

Culture Connection | Around the World

Strange Sports

Almost everyone knows about soccer, baseball, and basketball. But do you know anything about Octopush, Footvolley, or Pumpkin Regattas? Read about these strange sports and how they began!

Octopush

Octopush comes from England, but people now play it all over the world. A scuba diving club invented the game in 1954. During the winter, it was very cold to do scuba diving in the ocean, so they played Octopush in their swimming pool. It's a little like hockey, but people play it under water. Players use a small stick. They try to push a puck or 'squid' into a net to score points for their team. They called the game 'octo' – push because there were eight players. Unfortunately it isn't much fun to watch because you can't see the players!

24 Work with a partner. In which countries do you think these sports are popular? Match the sports to different countries. Choose from these or add your own.

Australia
France
New Zealand
United States of America
Canada
United Kingdom

1 baseball
2 cricket
3 soccer
4 rugby
5 ice hockey
6 cycling

25 Listen and read. When did people start these strange sports?

CONTENT WORDS
contest   court   net   puck   race   regatta   rowing   scuba diving   team

26 Look at 25. Read and say **true** or **false**.

1 You play Octopush in the ocean.
2 You can't see the players in a game of Octopush.
3 In Brazil, in 1965, people played soccer on the beach.
4 In Footvolley you can't use your hands.
5 There's only one Pumpkin Regatta each year.

Footvolley

Footvolley is a sport from Brazil. The game started on Copacabana beach in 1965. Soccer players weren't allowed to play soccer on the beach then. When the police came, they went to the beach volleyball courts and played there. They invented Footvolley. It's just like volleyball, but the players use a soccer ball. Players have to pass the ball to the other team over a high net. They can't touch the ball with their hands. People still play Footvolley on the beach today. It's very exciting, but very difficult! Many famous Brazilian soccer players also play Footvolley.

Pumpkin Regatta

In the fall, in parts of the United States and Canada, people join in a contest called a Pumpkin Regatta. It's like a boat race, but the players don't race in boats. They race in giant, hollowed out pumpkins! The pumpkin races started in 1999 in Windsor in Nova Scotia. A man there grew giant pumpkins, and he decided to use them for rowing. Soon other places wanted their own regattas, and pumpkin racing became very popular. The pumpkins weigh more than 450 kilograms. After the race, there's usually a pumpkin pie-eating contest.

27 Complete this chart about the sports.

	Octopush	Footvolley	Pumpkin Regatta
Where is it from?			
What is it?			
What sport(s) is it like?			
Why did it start?			

THINK BIG Why did these sports start in these places? Can you do these sports in other countries?

culture connection (strange sports) Unit 8 **139**

Writing | Combining Sentences with *and*, *but*, *or*

28 Complete these sentences. Then listen and check.

> I go to bed at 9:00 and wake up at 7:00.
> Dad eats cheese, but Mom doesn't eat cheese.
> We can go to the park or go to the movies.

and but or

1 I like eating olives, ? I don't like eating tomatoes.
2 I never clean my room ? take out the trash.
3 I get dressed at 7:15, ? I go to school at 8:30.

29 Join these sentences. Then write.

1 My sister plays tennis. My brother plays baseball. (*and*)
2 I usually eat eggs in the morning. This morning, I'm having pancakes. (*but*)
3 We can have chicken for dinner. We can try the new restaurant. (*or*)
4 There aren't any onions in the fridge. There are some green peppers. (*but*)
5 My dad works at a hospital. My mom works at a school. (*and*)

30 Read and choose.

I don't like playing sports, ¹**but/or** I need to get some exercise. I usually play video games after school, ²**but/or** I watch a DVD. My sister likes playing tennis ³**and/but** volleyball, but I don't. But I love going hiking with my family in the mountains. It's cool to see lots of animals ⁴**and/but** birds.

31 Write three sentences about healthy habits. Use *and*, *but*, and *or* once.

all, au, aw | Phonics

 32 Listen, read and repeat.

1 **all** 2 **au** 3 **aw**

 33 Listen and find. Then say.

b**all** h**au**l dr**aw**

 34 Listen and blend the sounds.

1 s-m-all small 2 c-all call
3 t-all tall 4 y-aw-n yawn
5 c-l-aw claw 6 w-all wall
7 l-aw law 8 P-aul Paul

 35 Read aloud. Then listen and chant.

I'm Paul, I'm bored.
Yawn, yawn.
Let's play, let's play
With a ball,
Let's draw, let's draw
A wall.

Values | Get exercise.

 **36 Look and listen. Point to and say the healthy activities.**

a  b  c  d

37 Work with a partner. Tell your partner to do healthy things.

 Don't watch TV. Go outside and play soccer!

Ride your bike at a park or in your neighborhood. It's fun, and it's good for you.

PROJECT

38 Work with a group. Think of a new game you can play outside. Write down the rules. Teach the rest of the class your new game.

Review

39 Read and choose. Then say.

1. Did she **eat/eating** a fruit salad at lunchtime?
2. **Did/Don't** you do any exercise yesterday?
3. Did they drink a lot of water today? No, they **did/didn't**.
4. Lenny is tired. He **didn't/don't** get enough sleep last night.

40 Do a survey of your classmates. Add two of your own questions. Ask and answer.

1. eat/healthy/food?
2. get/sleep/last night?
3. do/exercise/last week?
4. brush/teeth/this morning?
5. ride/bike/on the weekend?
6. drink/a lot of/water/today?
7. ?
8. ?

Did you get enough sleep last night?

Yes, I did.

41 Read and complete.

1. Mehmet ? (sleep) for twelve hours last night.
2. The cat ? (stop) drinking milk.
3. Mom and Dad ? (go) to the mountains on the weekend.
4. My friend ? (fall) out of a tree in the park yesterday.
5. I ? (join) the swim club today.
6. Anita ? (carry) my bag to school for me.

I Can

- talk about healthy and unhealthy habits.
- ask and answer about activities in the past.
- use *and*, *or*, and *but* in sentences.

Unit 9 School Trips!

 1 Listen, look, and say.

Top 8 places to visit!

1 museum
2 dairy farm
3 art gallery
4 national park
5 theater
6 zoo
7 concert hall
8 aquarium

 2 Listen, find, and say.   **3** Play a game.

4 Listen and sing. Did she visit the zoo?

Learning Out of School

I like going on school trips,
Learning out of school.
We go to lots of places.
They're interesting and cool!

Aquarium, theater, concert hall, and zoo,
We saw some great things.
There was lots to do!

**School trips. School trips.
They're a lot of fun.
School trips. School trips.
Let's go on one!**

Where did you go?
What did you see?
We went to the zoo, we saw a play,
We had a great time!

Chorus

5 Look at 1. Ask and answer.

It was a sunny day.

Yes, I did.

Did you go to a national park?

THINK BIG Why is it good to go on school trips?

Story

 6 Listen and read. Did Luke enjoy the trip?

A Cool Trip

"Hi, Luke. Hi, Amy. How was your trip today?"
"It was OK."
"It was fantastic!"

1 Amy and Luke went on a trip today.

"The Red Rock National Park is so cool!"

2 They went to a big park where there are very old rocks.

"What did you do there?"
"We learned about rocks. There are so many kinds of rocks, Mom!"

3 Their guide told them a lot of things about the rocks in the park.

"So did you like it?"
"Yes, I did. It was really interesting."

4 Amy liked the park.

7 **Read and answer.**

1. Where did Luke and Amy go on their trip?
2. What did they learn about?
3. Did Amy like the trip? Why/Why not?
4. Did Luke enjoy the trip? Why/Why not?
5. What did Amy get for Luke in the gift shop?

THINK BIG What national parks are there in your country? Why do we have national parks?

Language in Action

8 🎧 175 Listen and look at the sentences. Help Luke and Amy make more.

got   had   liked   learned

Where did | he | go | ?
He | went | to an aquarium | .
What did | they | do | ?
They | walked | a lot | .
They | didn't see | a penguin | .

9 Complete the chart. Then make new sentences.

did (x2)   didn't   go   saw   went

1	Where	did	they	?	?	They	went	to the zoo.
2	What	?	she	do	?	She	?	a play.
3		Did	you	like it	?	Yes, I	?	
4		Did	you	go to the museum	?	No, I	? go	to the museum.

Did you go to the zoo yesterday?

No, I didn't.

Language in Action

10 Match the verbs. Test your partner. Then make sentences.

1 go
2 have
3 get
4 eat
5 is
6 see

a ate
b saw
c had
d went
e got
f was

11 Use the verbs from 10 in the past. Then say.

1 Yesterday, I ? two bananas before school.
2 Susie ? you a present from the gift shop.
3 On the weekend, I ? a play at the theater.
4 The school trip ? great.
5 We ? a lot of fun on our trip to the zoo.
6 They ? to a national park on Friday.

12 Ask and answer. Use the words from the boxes.

last weekend   last year   yesterday

eat get go have is learn like see visit walk

Where did you go yesterday?

I went to the art gallery. It was fun.

language practice (*Where did you go? I went to the zoo.*) Unit 9

Content Connection | Art

13 Look at the paintings. Do you like them? Which is your favorite? Compare with a partner.

14 Listen and read. Then match paragraphs **1–4** to pictures **a–d**.

CONTENT WORDS

artist   colorful   funny   happy   impressionist   oil painting
painter   sad   sketch   strange   watercolor

a
The Little Giants by Francisco de Goya

b
Spring 1573 by Giuseppe Arcimboldo

c
Old Man with his Head in his Hands by Vincent Van Gogh

d
Haystacks at Giverny by Claude Monet

At the Art Gallery

1 **@Amylovesart** Last week, I went to the National Gallery with my mom. Was it boring? No way! Did you know there are lots of messages in paintings, and there are lots of different styles? This was my favorite painting. An Italian artist painted it in the 16th century. It looks like a face, doesn't it? It is, but it's also lots of other things. Every part of the face and body is a different spring fruit, vegetable, or flower. I like this picture because it's pretty, colorful, and smart. It shows humans and nature.

What are your favorite paintings? Please write and tell me.

2 **@ConchiConchi** I love this painting from the Prado Museum in Madrid. There are children in it. They're playing a funny game. The young children look happy, but the older children look a little tired. Mom says the artist painted it in the 19th century just before he stopped hearing. He went deaf. That's really sad. I think the painter became an artist for the king of Spain.

3 **@MattieMonstreParis** My grandmother has this painting in her living room. It isn't the original; someone copied it. A French impressionist painter painted the original, and it's in the Musée d'Orsay in Paris. Anyway this reminds me of summer. It's on a farm, probably. My grandmother says this is one of the painter's best paintings. He painted another twenty paintings like this with different colors. That's a little strange, isn't it?

4 **@MoniqueNetherlands** This is in a museum near my house in the Netherlands. It's by a Dutch painter. It isn't an oil painting, it's just a pencil sketch with watercolor. This painting is sad, but I think it's interesting. I mean, what's that man thinking? Why is he so sad? Maybe it's a little scary, too because maybe something horrible happened. The painter painted this in 1882. My dad says the painter was very sick. He was in the hospital with a mental illness.

@Amylovesart Wow! So many great paintings in museums all over the world. I'd like to see them one day!

15 Look at **14**. Answer the questions in your notebook.
1. Which painter painted for the king?
2. Which painter had an illness?
3. Which painter painted fruit and vegetable people?
4. Which painter painted a painting twenty times?

16 **Student A:** Close your book. Answer your partner's questions about Guiseppe Arcimbaldo and Vincent Van Gogh. What can you remember?

Student B: Close your book. Answer your partner's questions about Claude Monet and Francisco de Goya. What can you remember?

1. Where did he come from?
2. What did he paint?
3. When did he paint it?
4. What's interesting about the painting?
5. Do you like it?

Where did Vincent Van Gogh come from?

He came from the Netherlands.

Yes, that's right.

 **THINK BIG** What do you like to see most in paintings; people, animals, or nature? Why?

PROJECT

17 Find out about another famous painting. Then present it to the class.

I went to the National Gallery of Art in Washington, D.C. It's a famous art gallery. I saw a famous painting by Pierre-Auguste Renoir. It's called *A Girl with a Watering Can*. It was painted in 1876. I think it's a beautiful painting.

content connection (paintings) Unit 9

Grammar

18 **Look, listen, and read. Did Mary see the play?**

Bill: I didn't see you outside the theater last night. Where were you?

Mary: We were late. First, the car didn't start. Then we didn't catch the bus because we didn't get to the bus stop on time. We didn't arrive before the play started, so we didn't see any of the actors go into the theater.

Bill: But you saw the play.

Mary: No, we didn't. Dad didn't have the tickets. They were in the pocket of his other jacket!

I/You/He/She/It/We/They	**didn't** play. **didn't** walk. **didn't** stay.
I/You/He/She/It/We/They	**didn't** go. **didn't** see. **didn't** come.

19 Write sentences in your notebook.

1. The bus/not stop/at our bus stop.
2. The play/not start/at 5 o'clock.
3. Erol/not see/any actors.
4. George/not take/pictures.
5. They/not visit/the national park.
6. Dina and Eva/not like/the art gallery.

Grammar

20 The sentences are false. Correct them in your notebook.

1. Last summer, Tom went to Disneyland.
   Tom ? to Disneyland. He ? to Eurodisney.
2. Yesterday, May played tennis with Carmen.
   May ? tennis with Carmen. She ? tennis with Jenny.
3. Last week, Sam visited the London Aquarium.
   Sam ? the London Aquarium. He ? the Tower of London.
4. Last month, we learned about rocks at school.
   We ? about rocks at school. We ? about plants.
5. Three days ago, Eduardo saw a play.
   Eduardo ? a play. He ? a movie at the movie theater.
6. Hundreds of years ago, people watched TV.
   People ? TV. They ? shows or plays.

21 Read Amanda's list of vacation activities. In your notebook, write about the things she did and didn't do.

```
go to Ellis Island ✓
see the Statue of Liberty ✓
visit the Guggenheim museum ✓
travel to Yosemite national park ✗    eat dinner with Aunt Harriet ✗
get tickets for a Broadway show ✗     write postcards to friends ✗
go shopping ✓
```

22 Now close your books and try to remember. What did Amanda do? What didn't Amanda do? Use the words from the box for help.

> aquarium   art gallery   concert hall   go shopping
> meet Aunt Harriet   museum   national park   theater   zoo

23 Tell your partner about five things you did on vacation last year and five things you didn't do.

I went to the aquarium, but I didn't go to the museum.

I went to a farm. I saw lots of animals. I didn't go to the aquarium.

Culture Connection | Around the World

The World Stage

1   Today, people everywhere enjoy watching movies and television. But the TV and the movies are quite new. Before movies and television, people didn't have lots of entertainment. Instead they did things at home, or they sometimes went to theaters to see plays or performances. Watching performances on stage didn't stop being popular. Today around the world, different countries have different types of stage performances that were popular in the past and are popular today.

2   There were theaters in Greece more than 2,000 years ago. Most Greek cities had a theater. Greek plays were funny or sad, but all of them taught important lessons about life. In those times, all the actors were men or boys, and there was a chorus with people singing. Greek plays are still popular today, and every summer people enjoy watching them in open-air theaters.

24 Work with a partner and guess. When did these things happen? Match the sections to make sentences.

1	The first movie theater opened	the Moondog Coronation Ball in Cleveland, Ohio,	in 1765. They called it an animal menagerie.
2	The first zoo opened	in Vienna, Austria,	in 1952.
3	Families bought their first TVs in	in New Orleans,	in 1896. All the movies were silent.
4	The first rock concert was	in the U.S.,	in 1945. They cost $100.

25 Listen and read. Where did the first theater open?

CONTENT WORDS
dramatic   entertainment   flamenco   open-air theater
performance   play   popular   puppet   show   stage

26 Find these numbers in **25**. Complete the sentences.

1 2,000 years ago there ❓ .
2 In the 1600s, people ❓ .
3 Hundreds of years ago, flamenco ❓ .
4 In the 11th century, people from ❓ .

154 Unit 9

3   William Shakespeare made the theater popular in England about 400 years ago. Shakespeare wrote many plays. People laughed and cried when they watched them in the 1600s, and they still do today. Today you can see his plays in theaters all over the world in many different languages, and everybody loves them. One of his most famous plays is *Romeo and Juliet*.

4   Music and dance are also popular stage shows. In Spain, people love watching performances of flamenco dancing and music. Flamenco comes from Southern Spain. It started hundreds of years ago when people moved to Spain from the East. Usually there's a guitar, and men and women dance. 'Palmeros' clap in a special way with the dancers. Flamenco music and dance are very dramatic. Together, the music and dance tell a story.

5   In Vietnam, people enjoy watching an interesting kind of theater called Mua Roi Nuoc. There aren't any actors – only puppets. The puppets are on a stage filled with water. People from the Red River Delta began doing Mua Roi Nuoc puppet shows in the 11th century, but people still watch performances today. They're magical.

6   The TV and movies are a lot of fun, but stage performances made us happy through history, and they continue to make us smile or cry.

27 Read and choose the correct answer.

1 Greek plays were   a always sad.   b all about life.
2 Shakespeare was   a Greek.   b very popular.
3 Flamenco is a performance of   a music and dance.   b a long story.
4 The Mua Roi Nuoc puppets   a are very big.   b are on water.

28 Work with a partner. Ask and answer.

> going to concerts   going to the movies   going to the theater
> playing cards   playing musical instruments
> playing video games   singing with your family   watching TV

1 Which of the things in the box do you do in your free time?
2 What did people do in your country in the past in their free time?

THINK BIG Which do you prefer watching; dance, theater, or movies? Why?

culture connection (stage performances) Unit 9 **155**

Writing | Writing Sentences

29 **Read and find. Then listen and check.**

> Sentences have **subjects**, **verbs**, and **objects**. They appear in this order:
> **We** **had** fun.
> **They** **didn't see** a show.
> **Did** **you** **see** a sea lion show?

1 Did you visit a zoo?
2 Yes, I did.
3 I saw elephants and zebras.

30 **Find the subjects, verbs, and objects.**

1 Did she visit a dairy farm?
2 They didn't see any scary paintings.
3 I learned about rocks.
4 Did you see a movie?

31 **Put the words in order to make detail sentences.**

1 went | We | to the National Gallery.
2 old and new paintings. | saw | I
3 love | I | painting and listening to guides.
4 Our class | famous artists. | learned about

32 **Find the title, topic sentence, and final sentence. Now write the paragraph in your notebook.**

> It was lots of fun.   My favorite school trip
> We usually go on school trips every summer.

156 Unit 9

nt, ld, nd, st | Phonics

 33 Listen, read, and repeat.

1 **nt** 2 **ld** 3 **nd** 4 **st**

 34 Listen and find. Then say.

te**nt** chi**ld** ha**nd** ne**st**

 35 Listen and blend the sounds.

1 p-l-a-n-t   plant
3 c-o-l-d   cold
5 s-a-n-d   sand
7 ch-e-s-t   chest

2 o-l-d   old
4 b-a-n-d   band
6 a-n-t   ant
8 f-a-s-t   fast

 36 Read aloud. Then listen and chant.

An old, cold band
Playing in the sand.
A fast ant
Playing in a tent.

Values | Recognize your talents.

37 Complete the chart using the words from the box.

> basketball   dance   drawing   English   math   painting   science   soccer   swimming

a
b
c

Sports	Arts	School Subjects
?	?	?
?	?	?
?	?	?

38 Work with a partner. Talk about your talents.

 Do you like math?

 No, I don't. But I like art! I'm good at painting.

PROJECT

39 Have a **Talent Show**. Share your talent with the class.

Review

40 Look and say the places.

1  2  3  4

41 Complete the dialog. Then role-play.

A: Hey! How are you, Claudia?
B: I'm fine, Dad.
A: What did you ¹? today?
B: I ²? have lessons today. I ³? on a school trip with my class.
A: Cool! Where ⁴? you ⁵? ?
B: We went to the ⁶? .
A: That sounds fun. Did you ⁷? it?
B: Yes. I ⁸? . It ⁹? really fun, but I ¹⁰? see the monkeys. They were hiding!

42 Work with a partner. Plan your own school trip. Then present it to the class.

Where did you go?
What did you do?
What did you learn?
Did you like it?
Why/Why not?

> We went to a toy museum. We saw some very old toys. Some of them were a hundred years old! We liked it a lot.

I Can
- talk about actions in the past and places to visit.
- talk about paintings.
- write sentences with a subject, verb, and object.

Checkpoint | Units 7-9

How Well Do I Know It? Can I Use It?

1 Think about it. Read and draw. Practice.

😊 I know this.   😐 I need more practice.   😟 I don't know this.

#		PAGES			
1	**Food:** bread, mustard, onions, turkey…	112	😊	😐	😟
2	**Healthy habits:** ate breakfast, drank water, got enough sleep, rode my bike…	128	😊	😐	😟
3	**School trip places:** aquarium, museum, national park, theater…	144	😊	😐	😟
4	**School trip activities:** saw a penguin show, saw a movie, learned about rocks, saw a play…	145	😊	😐	😟
5	**Is** there **any** pizza? Yes, there is. There**'s some** pizza.	116–117	😊	😐	😟
6	**How much** food is there? There's **an** onion, **a lot of** meat, and **a little** ketchup. There aren't **many** potatoes.	120–121	😊	😐	😟
7	**Did** you **get** enough exercise? Yes, I **did**. **Did** you **get** enough sleep? No, I **didn't**.	132–133	😊	😐	😟
8	They **changed** clothes, and we **cleaned** the room. She **exercised**, and he **dropped** in.	136–137	😊	😐	😟
9	Where **did** they **go**? They **went** to the zoo.	148–149	😊	😐	😟
10	I **didn't call**, and he **didn't come**.	152–153	😊	😐	😟

I Can Do It!

2 Get ready.

A Complete the dialog with Kelly's answers. Then listen and check.

Kelly: Hello?
Dad: Hi, Kelly. It's Dad.
Kelly: Oh, hi, Dad!
Dad: How is New York City?
Kelly: ¹
Dad: What did you do yesterday?
Kelly: ²
Dad: That sounds fun. Did you like it?
Kelly: ³
Dad: Great. So, when is your soccer game?
Kelly: ⁴
Dad: I see. Did you get enough sleep last night?
Kelly: ⁵
Dad: That's good. Did you eat breakfast this morning?
Kelly: ⁶
Dad: That sounds delicious! Well, good luck today. Call me after your game.
Kelly: OK, Dad. Talk to you later.
Dad: Bye.

Kelly's answers

a Yes, Dad. I ate a big pancake.
b Yes, it was great! We saw a lot of interesting paintings.
c Yes, I went to bed at 7:00 last night.
d We went to the Museum of Modern Art.
e It's today. It starts at 2:00.
f It's really cool. We arrived yesterday afternoon.

B Practice the dialog in **A** with a partner. Make up your own answers.

Checkpoint | Units 7–9

3 Get set.

STEP 1 Cut out the cards on page 161 of your Workbook.

STEP 2 Read Dialog 1 below. Then place the cards in order to create Dialog 2.

STEP 3 Look at the pictures below. Choose the picture that illustrates each dialog. Now you're ready to **Go!**

4 Go!

A With a partner, practice Dialog 1. Change parts and practice again.

A: Where did you go yesterday?
B: We went to a big art gallery.
A: What did you do there?
B: We looked at some paintings.
A: Did you like it?
B: Not really. The paintings were strange.
A: What did you eat for dinner?
B: I ate a big pizza. It was delicious.
A: Did you get enough sleep last night?
B: No. I went to bed at 11:00.
A: Did you eat breakfast this morning?
B: No. I drank some water. I feel a bit sick.

> Where did you go yesterday?

> We went to a big art gallery.

B Use your cards to act out Dialog 2 with a partner.

5 **Write about yourself in your notebook.**

- Where did you go last weekend?
- What did you do there?
- Did you like it?
- What or who did you see?
- Did you get enough sleep last night?
- Did you eat a healthy breakfast?
- Did you get any exercise?

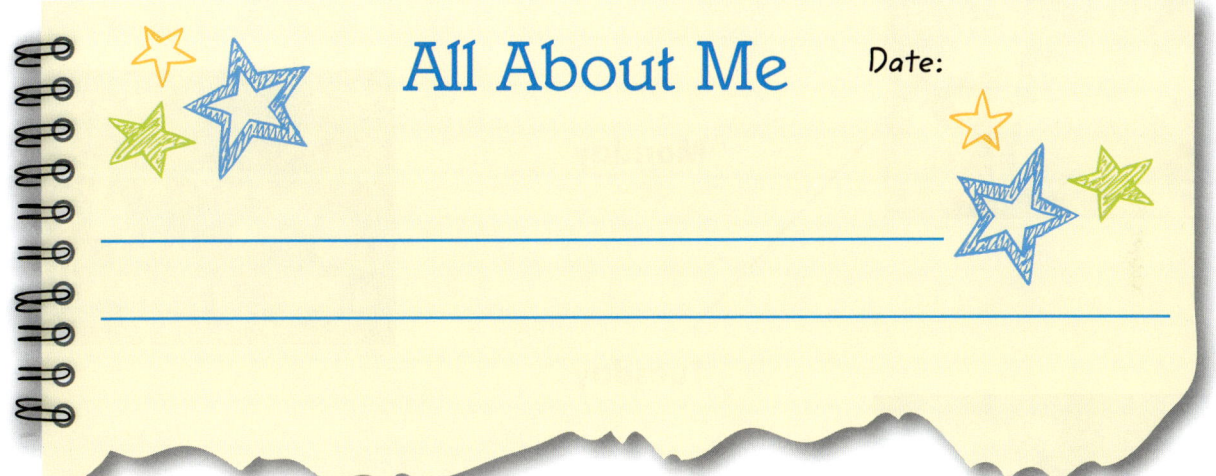

How Well Do I Know It Now?

6 **Think about it. Look at page 160 and your notebook. Draw again.**
  A **Use a different color.**
  B **Read and think.**
   I can ask my teacher for help.
   I can practice.

7 **Rate this Checkpoint.**

Checkpoint Units 7–9 **163**

Units 7–9 Exam Preparation

– Part A –

Look at the pictures. What did Alex do last week?
Listen and draw a line from the day to the correct picture.
There is one example.

Sunday

Monday

Tuesday

Wednesday

Thursday

Friday

Saturday

– Part B –

Look at the pictures and read the story. Write some words to complete the sentences about the story. You can use 1, 2, or 3 words.

Jane lives with her parents and her sister, Lily, near a national park. Janes likes riding her bike in the forest there. Last Sunday, Jane and her family went for a walk after lunch. They saw a woman. She was painting flowers. "That's very nice!" said Jane, and the woman smiled.

Examples

Jane's sister is named ____Lily____.
Jane's house is close to a __national park__.

Questions

1 Last Sunday, Jane had lunch and went for a _____ in the forest.
2 There was a _____ who was painting in the forest.
3 Jane thought the painting of the flowers was _____.

Jane talked to her uncle the next day. "Do you want to come to the art gallery with me, Jane?" he asked. They went to the art gallery that afternoon. The woman from the forest was there, too! "Welcome to my art gallery!" she said. Jane saw the painting with the flowers again. She really liked it, so the woman gave it to her. Now the painting is in Jane's bedroom.

4 Jane's uncle invited her to _____.
5 The woman gave Jane a _____.
6 Jane put the painting in her _____.

Wordlist

Find these words in your language. Then write in your notebook.

Unit 1	Page
do my homework	4
eat breakfast	4
get dressed	4
go home	4
go to school	4
go to the park	4
play soccer	4
play video games	4
wake up	4
watch TV	4
seven thirty	5
time	5
brush your teeth	6
face	6
morning	6
like	7
put on his shoes	7
afternoon	8
evening	8
seven fifty	8
eat dinner	9
ride my bike	9
bacteria	10
cough	10
decay	10
germ	10
gum disease	10
health	10
healthy	10
skin	10
sneeze	10
sweat	10
take a shower	10
wash your hands	10
dark	14
different	14
globe	14
half-turn	14
map	14
time zone	14
chat	15
e-pals	15
online	15
subject	16
verb	16
bone	17
cake	17
note	17
shape	17

Unit 2	Page
cashier	20
farmer	20
firefighter	20
nurse	20
police officer	20
scientist	20
student	20
waiter	20
farm	21
fire station	21
hospital	21
laboratory	21
police station	21
college	21
school	24
create	26
drawing	26
fashion designer	26
gallery	26
material	26
painting	26
pattern	26
photographer	26
photo shoot	26
piece of art	26
professional	26
sculpture	26
sketch	26
unusual	26
donate	30
be proud of	31
collect	31
community	31
contest	31
get lost	31
Spain	31
trash	31
skates	33
ski	33
smart	33
smile	33
smoke	33
space	33
spoon	33
star	33
stop	33
storm	33

Unit 3	Page
clean my room	36
do the dishes	36
feed the fish	36
make my bed	36
practice the piano	36
study for a test	36
take out the trash	36
walk the dog	36
always	37
chores	37

day	37	pay	49	tree frog	64
twins	37	ray	49	canary	68
sometimes	37	soy	49	goldfish	68
say	38	toy	49	million	68
alarm clock	39			parakeet	68
never	39	**Unit 4**	**Page**	rodent	68
usually	41	animal	58	alligator	69
adult	42	bear	58	gecko	69
amount	42	camel	58	hamster	69
cash	42	deer	58	snake	69
cents	42	lizard	58	tarantula	69
clean	42	owl	58	topic sentence	70
cost	42	penguin	58	bean	71
dollar	42	sea lion	58	boil	71
earn	42	shark	58	coin	71
let (someone) know	42	toucan	58	foe	71
pocket money	42	desert	59	meat	71
save	42	forest	59	oil	71
stranger	42	ice and snow	59	peach	71
subtotal	42	jungle	59	tea	71
times a week	42	lake	59	toe	71
total	42	mountain	59		
wash	42	ocean	59	**Unit 5**	**Page**
business	46	rain forest	59	cloudy	74
entrance	46	trick	60	cold	74
goat	46	well	60	cool	74
noodles	46	blend in	64	hot	74
pavement	46	bottom of the ocean	64	rainy	74
share	46	camouflage	64	snowy	74
shovel	46	chameleon	64	sunny	74
task	46	eat	64	today	74
tiring	46	polar bear	64	warm	74
capital letters	48	rock	64	windy	74
title	48	stone	64	coat	75
boy	49	stonefish	64	sweater	75
joy	49	surroundings	64	raincoat	75
May	49	tree bark	64	sandals	75

wordlist Units 3–5

Wordlist

scarf	75	horrible	90	plant	103
shorts	75	look	90	play	103
sunglasses	75	nice	90	plum	103
hike	76	pie	90		
snack	76	smell	90	**Unit 7**	**Page**
yesterday	76	soft	90	bread	112
average	80	sound	90	cucumbers	112
climate	80	soup	90	from	112
degrees Celsius	80	sweet	90	green	112
dry	80	taste	90	lettuce	112
extreme	80	terrible	90	mushrooms	112
mild	80	tight	90	olives	112
minus	80	danger	93	onions	112
temperature	80	avoid	96	peppers	112
tourist	80	brain	96	tomato sauce	112
sleep	81	echo	96	turkey	112
cricket	84	fresh	96	fridge	114
kite	84	information	96	surprise	114
fill up	85	senses	96	blood	118
sledding	85	sound waves	96	bone	118
snowball fight	85	taste buds	96	brain	118
detail sentences	86	tongue	96	energy	118
swim	86	smelly	100	fat/water soluble	118
scar	87	clean	101	iron	118
scout	87	stink	101	muscle	118
slim	87	take care of	101	teeth	118
slow	87	wet	101	vitamin	118
snail	87	final sentence	102	blueberries	122
swan	87	black	103	hard-boiled/fried	
sweet	87	block	103	eggs	122
		blow	103	cereal	122
Unit 6	**Page**	flag	103	honey	122
awful	90	flip-flops	103	oats	122
beautiful	90	fly	103	porridge	122
delicious	90	glad	103	toast	122
feel	90	glass	103	donut	123
flowers	90	glow	103	butter	124

maple syrup	124	contest	139	impressionist	150
pancake	124	court	139	Italian	150
brick	125	footvolley	139	oil painting	150
cream	125	pumpkin	139	painter	150
cry	125	race	139	scary	150
dream	125	rowing	139	sketch	150
drive	125	claw	141	strange	150
frog	125	draw	141	watercolor	150
grass	125	haul	141	entertainment	154
prince	125	tall	141	open-air theater	154
prize	125	wall	141	performance	154
troll	125	yawn	141	play	154
				popular	154
Unit 8	**Page**	**Unit 9**	**Page**	dramatic	155
any	128	aquarium	144	flamenco	155
enough	129	art gallery	144	show	155
unhealthy	130	concert hall	144	stage	155
bad	131	dairy farm	144	Vietnam	155
active	134	museum	144	object	156
activities	134	national park	144	ant	157
body	134	school trip	144	band	157
burn	134	theater	144	chest	157
calorie	134	zoo	144	child	157
in shape	134	had	145	cold	157
measure	134	interesting	145	fast	157
put on weight	134	saw	145	nest	157
rest	134	went	145	sand	157
all	134	learned	146	tent	157
hockey	138	liked	146	English	158
net	138	old	146		
octopush	138	got	147		
puck	138	walked	147		
regatta	138	ate	149		
scuba diving	138	artist	150		
team	138	boring	150		
ball	139	Dutch	150		
call	139	French	150		

Big English Song

From the mountaintops to the bottom of the sea,
From a big blue whale to a baby bumblebee –
If you're big, if you're small, you can have it all,
And you can be anything you want to be!

**It's bigger than you. It's bigger than me.
There's so much to do, and there's so much to see!
The world is big and beautiful, and so are we!
Think big! Dream big! Big English!**

So in every land, from the desert to the sea,
We can all join hands and be one big family.
If we love, if we care, we can go anywhere!
The world belongs to everyone; it's ours to share.

**It's bigger than you. It's bigger than me.
There's so much to do, and there's so much to see!
The world is big and beautiful, and so are we!
Think big! Dream big! Big English!**

**It's bigger than you. It's bigger than me.
There's so much to do, and there's so much to see!
The world is big and beautiful and waiting for me.
A one, two, three…
Think big! Dream big! Big English!**

Pearson Education Limited
Edinburgh Gate
Harlow
Essex CM20 2JE
England
and Associated Companies throughout the world.
www.pearsonelt.com/bigenglish

© Pearson Education Limited 2015

Authorised adaptation from the United States edition entitled Big English, 1st Edition, by Mario Herrera and Christopher Sol Cruz. Published by Pearson Education Inc. © 2013 by Pearson Education, Inc.

The right of Mario Herrera and Christopher Sol Cruz to be identified as the authors of this Work have been asserted by them in accordance with the Copyright, Designs and Patents Act 1988.

All rights reserved; no part of this publication may be reproduced, stored in a retrieval system, or transmitted in any form or by any means, electronic, mechanical, photocopying, recording, or otherwise without the prior written permission of the Publishers.

First published 2015
Sixth impression 2018
ISBN: 978-1-4479-8938-7
Set in Heinemann Roman
Printed in Italy by L.E.G.O. S.p.A.

Acknowledgements

The publisher would like to thank the following for their kind permission to reproduce photographs:

(Key: b-bottom; c-centre; l-left; r-right; t-top)

123RF.com: belchonock 50r, blinztree 126 (noodles), Brian Jackson 104/37 (centre left), Cathy Yeulet 47tr, Charles Brutlag 104/37 (right), cokemomo 126/37 (bottom left), Ferli Achirulli 27t, Gennadiy Poznyakov 158tc, hans slegers 88 (sunscreen), Igor Zakharevich 88 (sunglasses), Ivanka Filipova 126/37 (bottom right), jesus David carballo prieto 69 (spider), Leah-Anne Thompson 98t, Michael Pettigrew 66, minadezhda 122tr, Nagy-Bagoly Ilona 158b, Olga Volodina 88tc, racorn 142 (b), Richard Martin Lee 126 (rice), Siarhei Baryliuk 42 (half dollar), Tatiana Popova, waldru 104/35 (right); **Age Fotostock Spain S.L.:** Allesalltag Bildagentur 36/6, Dan Bannister 10ltl, **Alamy Images:** a. collection 122 (Yoko), allesalltag 18c, Barry Bland 138l, CandyBox Images 9l, 21bl, 25bl, 62l, 81tl, 91bl, 99l, 104cl, 117bl, 127bl, 129br, 143br, 145bl, 148l, 153br, William Caram 31tl, David Kneafsey 20/2, Deco, Directphoto Collection 20/6, epa european pressphoto agency b.v. 138r, fStop Images GmbH 20/3, Geoffrey Robinson 21 (d), Brian Hickey 26t, Iain Sarjeant 21 (b), Image Source 4/2, 12r, 128, José Manuel Gelpi Díaz 4/6, LH Images 21 (c), MARKA 144/5, Martin Wierink 112 (sandwich), MBI 8r, 21br, 32br, 40br, 47br, 59br, 62r, 69 (Jed), 79b, 85br, 95br, 101br, 104cr, 113br, 127br, 129bl, 135t, 143bl, 149br, MIXA 124c, Paul Doyle 21tr, PhotoStock-Israel 44l, Radharc Images 21 (f), Tetra Images 36/1, Ulrich Doering 84r, Visions of America, LLC 134, Zoonar GmbH 81br; **Bridgeman Art Library Ltd:** 150 (c), 150 (d), Giraudon 150 (a), 150 (b); **Corbis:** 2 / Eri Morita / Ocean 144/1, 68 / Ocean 120b, David Buffington / Blend Images 4/4, Denisa Haldova / Moodboard 142 (c), Lane Oatey / Blue Jean Images 84l, Randy Faris 144/3, **Digital Vision:** 58/8, 73bl; **DK Images:** Peter Cross 58/2, Jules Selmes 118r, Simon Smith 119 (C), 121 (tomatoes), Clive Streeter 122 (d), William Shaw 112/3; **Fotolia.com:** Alena Ozerova 4/1, Andres Rodriguez 36/3, Angela Köhler 80br, apops 20/4, AVAVA 25 (a), Azaliya 69 (hamster), bkhphoto 88 (water), Blend Images 25 (c), 34r, bst2012 123 (Camilla), chawalitpix 69 (gecko), chrissycopelia 104/37 (centre right), coolmintpro 18r, DragonImages 26b, dule964 68bl, 69 (budgie), 72 (parrot), elnavegante 58/7, 73br, EPSTOCK 21 (a), erectus 64 (d), fothoss 74/1, galam 4/10, gitusik 4/9, Goinyk Volodymyr 58/6, 72 (penguin), Joe Gough 122 (c), helenlbuxton 122 (e), Herby (Herbert) Me 74/5, Hunta 47tl, Ints 46, iofoto 25 (b), 34l, ispstock 95t, Eric Isselée 68br, 69 (rabbit), ivanukh 152, Michael JELL 64 (a), karandaev 68tl, Konovalov Pavel 88 (hat), Alexey Kuznetsov 69 (snake), lacroix 118l, 119 (D), 121 (milk & eggs), Julien Leblay 80tl, Lucky Dragon 142 (d), Malyshchyts Viktar 112/10, mario beaugard 58/1, 72 (bear), Markus Bormann 37, Michael Flippo 36/2, Monkey Business 136, Natika 117bl, oriori 112/2, Ornitolog82 58/5, 63, 72 (lizard), paul_brighton 126 (dumplings), photka 50l, PiLensPhoto 81bl, PT Images 123 (Tony), rakjung2 73t, Reddogs 59t, robynmac 119 (E), 121 (green vegetables), Sanjay Deva 15 (Marcus), Serggod 91tr, .shock 21 (e), sueg0904 72 (dingo), travelwitness 21 (h), tupatu76 74/3, uwimages 119 (B), 121 (pasta), valery121283 119 (A), 121 (carrots), Valua Vitaly 15 (John), wolive 64 (b), xalanx 88tl, Yuri Arcurs 20/7, 32t; **Getty Images:** A DAGLI ORTI 155t, Blend Images / Hill Street Studios 28, Blend Images / KidStock 98b, Boston Globe 139, E+ / Juanmonino 36/4, Antony Giblin / Lonely Planet Images 30r, iStock / 360 / Nordroden 82l, iStock Vectors / Brandon Laufenberg 14, Lonely Planet Images / Brent Winebrenner 126/37 (top right), Photodisc / ColorBlind 18l, The Image Bank / David Young-Wolff 4/5; **Newscom:** Michael Snell; Robert Harding 10ltr, Zero Creatives 85t; **Pearson Education:** 106br, 112/9, 119br, 126 (boy), 127t, 142bl, 149tr, 153bl; **Pearson Education Ltd:** Jon Barlow 2ltl, 40/1, 43b, 69 (Isabella), Gareth Boden 144/6, Trevor Clifford 5bl, 11tl, 25br, 43tl, 54, 65r, 117br, 123bl, Jules Selmes 123 (Luis); **Photolibrary.com:** Creatas 11bc, ppfoto13 88 (gloves); **Shutterstock.com:** anawat sudchanham 82r, Andreas Gradin 105/2, Andrjuss 112/7, Apollofoto 9r, 24r, 40/2, 78l, 81tr, 83b, 89l, 91br, 99r, 117tl, 132l, 137l, 145br, 148r, 151tr, 158cr, ARENA Creative 26c, Stacy Barnett 31bl, Casey K. Bishop, bonchan 122 (a), 122 (b), Charles Brutlag 64 (c), carroteater 42 (one dollar), Cathy Keifer 97l, 105b, cellistka 72 (snake), crshelare 58/3, Darren Baker 16, David Steele 58/4, 73c, Denizo71 36/5, Diego Cervo 100r, Digital Media Pro 4/7, Dmitry Kalinovsky 86b, Dmitry Naumov 142 (a), dwphotos 154-155b, Erasmus Wolff 35, Eric Isselee 72 (koala), 96br, Erika Cross 31br, evka119 42t, fenghui 21 (g), Fotokostic 158tl, Gareth Leung 72 (kookaburra), GekaSkr 91/5 (2), 105/4, Gelpi JM 91/5 (3), Goodluz 20/5, 69 (Ethan), Graca Victoria 5br, 11tr, 24l, 32bl, 40bl, 47bl, 59bl, 65l, 69 (Sandra), 79t, 85bl, 89r, 108, 113bl, 117tr, 135l, 142br, 149tl, 151b, greenland 36/7, hartphotography 5t, 11br, 52, holbox 104/35 (centre), HomeArt 154tr, idiz 72 (kangaroo), iko 91/5 (5), Ingrid Petitjean 80bl, Ivaschenko Roman 112/6, Ivonne Wierink 10r, Jacek Chabraszewski 122 (Katie), 123 (Katie), Jaimie Duplass 75, 88tr, 106t, James Steidl 158tr, Jorg Hackemann 129t, kamonrat 70, kccullenPhoto 126/37 (top left), Kokhanchikov 91/5 (4), 105/1, 106bl, Kotenko Oleksandr 74/2, kwokfai 96bl, Ljupco Smokovski 100l, Lyudmila Suvorova 112 (pizza), Marcio Jose Bastos Silva 153t, Rob Marmion 11bl, 12l, 15 (Kara), Mat Hayward 91c, Matthew Bechelli 123br, Matthew Jacques 144/2, Mau Horng 10c, 124t, Michal Bednarek 31tr, Monkey Business Images 29, 120t, 143t, NaughtyNut 30l, Petr Malyshev 88 (umbrella), Phil MacD Photography 144/4, Pierre-Yves Babelon 74/4, 83t, 86t, R Gino Santa Maria 154-155 (curtain), Tom Reichner 96tr, Rich Carey 58/9, rsooll 42 (five cents), Rus S 105/3, Selfiy 154tl, Sergey Toronto 80tr, shupian 104/35 (left), sianc 104/37 (left), Smileus 10l, sniegirova mariia 91tl, Solphoto 91/5 (1), stefanolunardi 4/8, 79c, Stuart Miles 4/3, Tischenko Irina 68tr, 69 (goldfish), tobkatrina 48t, Tom Wang 20/8, tororo reaction 144/8, 160c, Ultrashock 72 (lion), Valentyn Volkov 124b, Viktor Gladkov 42b, Vlad61 58-59 (background), Vladimir Mucibabic 44r, Vladimir Wrangel 42 (one cent), wavebreakmedia 105/5, xavier gallego morell 95c, yalayama 8l, 27b, 43tr, 78r, 95bl, 97r, 101bl, 132r, 137r, 149bl, 151tl, 158cl, 159, Lisa F. Young 15 (Maria), 20/1, 48b, Yuri Arcurs 140, 145t, 160r, Zaneta Baranowska 112/5; **SuperStock:** Blend Images 40/3, 113t, 160l, Juniors 36/8, Photononstop 144/7

Cover Images: Front: **Shutterstock.com:** Pierre-Yves Babelon c, monticello l, restyler r

All other images © Pearson Education

Every effort has been made to trace the copyright holders and we apologise in advance for any unintentional omissions. We would be pleased to insert the appropriate acknowledgement in any subsequent edition of this publication.

Illustrated by

Tiago Americo, Sean@KJA-Artists, Victor Moshpoulos, Zaharias Papadopoulos (hyphen), Remy Simard, Christos Skaltsas (hyphen).